Adults with learning difficulties
Education for choice & empowerment

Adults with learning difficulties

Education for choice & empowerment

A handbook of good practice

Jeannie Sutcliffe

The National Institute of Adult Continuing Education
in association with
The Open University Press

Published by the National Institute of Adult Continuing Education
19B De Montfort Street, Leicester LE1 7GE, UK
In association with the Open University Press
Celtic Court, 22 Ballmoor, Buckingham MK18 1XW

Reprinted 1991, 1992, 1993, 1998

British Library Cataloguing in Publication Data
Sutcliffe, Jeannie
Adults with learning difficulties: education for choice and empowerment
1. Learning disordered persons. Remedial education
I. Title
371.9
ISBN 0-335-09609-3

Library of Congress Cataloging in Publication Data
Sutcliffe, Jeannie, 1958-
Adults with learning difficulties: education for choice and empowerment/Jeannie Sutcliffe
Includes bibliographical references and index.
ISBN 0-335-09609-3
1. Adult education–Great Britain.   2. Learning disabilities–Great Britain.   I. Title
LC5256.G7S975   1990
374´.941–dc20   90–41522
                                                                                                        CIP

Photoset in Garamond by Communitype Communications Ltd, Leicester
Designed by Stanley Sheard
Printed and bound in Great Britain by
Biddles Ltd, Guildford and King's Lynn

Contents

ACKNOWLEDGEMENTS

The NIACE Rowntree project was ably supported by the following people, to whom thanks are due:

Steering Committee

Sue Brown, *District Manager, Disability Services, Norfolk Social Services*
Ann Craft, *Lecturer, Nottingham University*
Maggy Crook, *Special Needs Development Officer, Avon*
Bernard Godding, *Area Head of Adult Education, Norfolk*
Matthew Griffiths, *National Education Officer, MENCAP*
Professor Malcolm Johnson, *Director, Department of Health and Social Welfare, The Open University*
Professor Chris Kiernan, *Director, Hester Adrian Research Centre, University of Manchester*
Andrea Linell, *Development Officer, The Rathbone Society, Leicester*
Joan Rush, *Senior Project Officer, King's Fund Centre*
Chris Vickerman, *Service Development Officer, Southwark Consortium*
Linda Ward, *Secretary, Disability Programme, Joseph Rowntree Foundation*

Project secretarial assistant: Anne Agius

Special thanks also to: Gary Bourlet, Shiela Carlton, Jane Colebourne, Helen Fletcher, John Hersov, Linda Hiscott, Peter Lavender, Stephen Macdonald, Carolyn Kewley, The Talking Together Group, Alan Tuckett, Andrea Whittaker, Paul Williams, and everyone who contributed time, ideas, information and photographs.

The Joseph Rowntree Foundation funds a programme of applied research and development projects in the broad fields of housing, social policy and social care, including disability. For further information on the Foundation's Disability Programme, contact Dr Linda Ward, c/o Norah Fry Research Centre, University of Bristol, 32 Tyndall's Park Road, Bristol BS8 1PY, tel: 0272 238164.

Foreword

I welcome the opportunity to write the foreword for a handbook which aims to disseminate good practice in the continuing education of adults with learning difficulties. I am sure this handbook will be a welcome addition for those working in adult, further and higher education. Professionals in the social services and working for health authorities, educationalists and families will find straightforward guidance and advice in it and many suggestions for new initiatives.

Within the 1944 Education Act (as amended by the 1988 Education Reform Act), Local Education Authorities are required to make suitable further education provision for the population in their area, including adults with learning difficulties. The handbook will be helpful to agencies and institutions as they plan the provision of opportunities for this important group of clients. It is of great importance that people with learning difficulties should be helped both practically and imaginatively to take their place in the community. Education provides the opportunities for integration, development of self-advocacy skills and attainment of independence and there are many examples of innovative approaches to this work. Good progress in this field depends upon full co-operation between all the agencies involved.

Alan Howarth
PARLIAMENTARY UNDER-SECRETARY OF STATE
DEPARTMENT OF EDUCATION AND SCIENCE

1. Using this handbook

WHO IS IT FOR?

This handbook has been written for people working in a teaching or enabling role with adults who have learning difficulties. They include:

- tutors and volunteers in adult, further and higher education

- staff working in day centres or day services run by social services departments, health authorities or voluntary organisations

- planners and managers of services, whose needs are addressed specifically in Chapter 10.

In addition, the handbook may also be a useful resource for:

- staff working in residential settings with people who have learning difficulties

- teachers working with young adults with moderate or severe learning difficulties in leavers' units at special schools

- relatives of people with learning difficulties.

DEFINITION OF TERMS

A deliberate decision has been taken to use the term 'people with learning difficulties' throughout this book. The term 'learning difficulties' has been increasingly adopted to overcome the stigma attached to the label 'mental handicap'.

The terms 'tutor' and 'student' have been used throughout. However, we recognise that people in agencies other than adult education may use different descriptions for those in the enabling and learning roles.

SETTING THE SCENE

It is estimated that between two and three per cent of the population have a learning difficulty. The range of learning difficulties is broad, from mild or moderate learning difficulties, to severe or profound and multiple learning difficulties. The learning difficulties tag must take second place to the notion that people are individuals — people first. It is no surprise that many self advocacy groups, which enable people with learning difficulties to speak up and to effect changes, are called 'People First'.

People's quality of life is affected by their experiences. For people with learning difficulties, life experiences can be limited in terms of opportunities for education, employment, leisure and other activities.

The National Institute of Adult Continuing Education upholds the views of the Independent Development Council as expressed in *Living Like Other People*:

- all people have the same value and therefore the same human rights

- people with learning difficulties should be part of the community and not segregated from society

- people with learning difficulties should be treated as individuals with needs and wishes which should be respected

- people with learning difficulties should be enabled to make informed choices and to take reasonable risks.

According to the Independent Development Council, services for adults with learning difficulties should:

- be based on and cater for specific individual needs and preferences

- actively promote the integration of all people

- be provided in places which other members of society use and value (for example colleges of further education, sports centres, workplaces)

- provide the full range of options available to adults without disabilities (for example employment, further education, volunteer work, leisure activities).

THE RANGE OF SERVICES FOR ADULTS WITH LEARNING DIFFICULTIES

This outline is designed to give a brief overview rather than a comprehensive list. Health authorities and social services departments are major providers, and, while services vary slightly from area to area, in general terms the following are to be found:

- Long-stay hospitals which are being gradually run down and closed. Despite community care initiatives, over 30,000 people remain in NHS hospitals.

- Social education centres (still called Adult Training Centres in some

areas), which are day centres run by social services departments.

- Hostels and group homes offering residential accommodation.

- Community teams of social workers and nurses, who offer field work services.

- Allied professionals working for the health authority, who offer specialist skills such as psychology, speech therapy, occupational therapy or physiotherapy.

In addition, a number of voluntary organisations (such as MENCAP, Barnardos, The National Autistic Society, The Rathbone Society) offer various forms of provision. The number of private homes is increasing: standards in those which have more than three residents are monitored by Social Services Registrations Officers. Employment Training caters for people with special educational needs, while Jobcentres have officers with responsibility for people with disabilities.

Local Education Authority Continuing Education

College-based provision for 16—19-year-olds with moderate learning difficulties has been established in many areas. The Further Education Unit staff development pack *From Coping to Confidence* raised awareness of this area. Provision for school leavers with severe learning difficulties is developing gradually, and is supported by the Further Education Unit publication *New Directions*. Continuing education for adults with learning difficulties was recommended in the Warnock Report (1978), which pointed out that resources spent on education would, in the long term, reduce dependence on other providers, such as health and social services. The report stated that: 'Existing provision in further education ... has developed in a piecemeal and unco-ordinated fashion. We consider that opportunities in further education should be increased and a coherent pattern of provision developed.'

To date, little has changed in terms of continuing education for adults with learning difficulties beyond the age of 19. Provision is far from being coherent and well planned.

HIGHLIGHTING GOOD PRACTICE: THE NIACE ROWNTREE PROJECT

The broad aims of the NIACE Rowntree Project, set up in 1988 by the National Institute of Adult Continuing Education with backing from the Joseph Rowntree Foundation, are outlined in the following sections.

A Network of Providers

Local Education Authorities, social services departments, health authorities and major voluntary organisations were invited to share details of learning opportunities for adults with learning difficulties. A named contact for the project was established in every Local Education Authority in England and Wales. The names, job titles and telephone numbers of these people are listed in NIACE's *Yearbook*, available from NIACE in Leicester.

Documenting Good Practice

Based on the details of provision received, a programme of visits was carried out to incorporate a range of:

● agency

● learning difficulties

● geographical area

● learning activity.

This handbook summarises, under broad, thematic headings, the positive aspects of learning taking place. It also highlights the gaps in provision which became apparent.

The case studies used to illustrate the text were current at the time of writing. The handbook case studies should be seen as valid examples of good practice 'trapped in amber'. It must be acknowledged that situations, circumstances and staff will change.

Documenting good practice in the education of the wider community about issues relating to people with learning difficulties proved most challenging. Public education is an important but highly sensitive issue. The information and ideas gathered are described in Chapter 9.

HOW TO USE THIS HANDBOOK

Readers should feel free to dip selectively into chapters of interest. Chapters 1—9 contain:

● case studies drawn from the project

● 'think for yourself' boxes designed to prompt readers to reflect on their local situations and to consider improvements

- recommendations
- listings of resources and suggested further reading.

Chapter 10 is aimed particularly at managers and planners, as well as practitioners. It contains a self-completion questionnaire which provides a framework for future developments.

The handbook presents a range of learning activities which are based on a student-centred approach. It is not prescriptive and does not offer tidy solutions or checklists. Neither is it a directory. Instead it invites readers to think about ways of working which open up new opportunities for students with learning difficulties to direct their learning — and their lives.

LEARNING IN ACTION

Education for adults with learning difficulties is a developing field. The contribution of adult continuing education to the development of people with learning difficulties is wide ranging. Examples include:

- Continuation of learning opportunities post-19, after statutory education has finished.

- Adult education as a partner in care in the community initiatives, providing learning opportunities for people with learning difficulties who are making the transition to community living.

- Opportunities for integration into a varied range of adult education activities.

- Dovetailing with other agencies to widen the overall range of learning activities offered.

- Providing learning support at critical periods — whether students are learning to adjust to a new living situation or facing retirement.

- Learning for work, leisure or personal development.

- Acting as a catalyst for the development of self advocacy work.

PORTRAITS OF STUDENTS WITH LEARNING DIFFICULTIES

The following profiles of students demonstrate the way in which learning has enriched or changed the lives of adults with learning difficulties. Education offers an active force in enabling people to take control of their lives — whether in terms of coping more independently, learning new skills or learning to communicate and to voice opinions.

John Ross is in his mid-forties and attends a social services day centre part-time. He grew up in the Midlands, where he worked on a farm for seven years. He moved to the south of England with his father, where they shared a flat. When John's father died several years ago, John decided to keep the flat on by himself. John has been regularly attending adult education classes. He has improved his reading and has developed good budgeting skills. He is proud of the way he manages to shop and cook for himself. A home help comes in regularly to give a hand with housework. John enjoys the social contact of education classes: 'It gives me something to do and gets me out of the house.' He has had a chance to get involved in new learning activities, to include drama, self advocacy and craft. He feels that the educational support he gets from adult education is of help to him. 'It keeps me going, coming here. I don't need the social workers as much.'

William Gadd is in his late sixties. Most of his life has been spent in institutions. Until a year ago he was living in a long-stay psychiatric hospital, where a group of older men with learning difficulties had been inappropriately placed. Before that he had lived in a hostel and in another long-stay hospital. Now he is living in a town-based residential unit for elderly people. Adult education tutors have been involved in William's latest move, working closely with hospital staff and social services staff. William has learnt to experience choice and decision-making. Everyday experiences — visiting supermarkets, catching a bus, making a cup of tea — have been new situations for William, who has learnt to adapt well. He has cast off his institutional clothes and has chosen for himself a set of bright new clothing. A yellow shirt and matching scarf are particular favourites. He has learnt the way to the shops and how to buy his cigarettes. He has developed a keen interest in cookery and is learning to make new recipes of his choice. William is fond of birds and feeds them every day.

He has learnt about them from books borrowed from the local library.

Sarita Patel is in her mid-twenties. She was born in India and came to live in England in her early teens. She has grasped English well, and speaks it in addition to her first language, which is Hindi. Sarita was referred by a psychologist to a school for children with severe learning difficulties. On leaving, she went to a social services day centre where light industrial work took up most of the week. She attended adult education classes in English as a Second Language, in which she and her mother learnt side by side. Sarita subsequently joined a general education group. She has learnt about the use of money and shopping. She has also developed her reading and writing skills. At one stage, an adult education tutor worked jointly with a community nurse on a programme designed to enable Sarita to be more independent in the community, which involved catching buses and finding the way around the town centre. Sarita expressed a clear interest in working with children. The adult education tutor facilitated a work experience placement for Sarita working with pre-school children in a nursery. Her confidence blossomed, and she has developed from a shy person with eyes downcast to a confident, mature young woman. She has recently joined a yoga evening class.

Stephen Morris has cerebral palsy, which has affected his mobility and co-ordination. He walks determinedly but awkwardly, often falls over but is resolute in his determination to get where he wants to go — independently. Stephen was referred to adult education by the Spastics Society. He had been throwing items around, although not at people. It was felt that much of his frustration arose from a difficulty in communicating. Stephen's speech was very unclear. He had basic literacy skills, and was offered the chance to use a Canon Communicator, on which messages can be typed. A speech therapist and an adult education tutor liaised and worked individually with Stephen at home to improve his confidence in using the communication aid. His behaviour improved as his communication skills grew. At first Stephen was adamant that he wanted only one to one tuition at home. After a few months, he expressed the wish to join an education group. This was arranged and for two years he worked on improving his reading, writing and spelling in a group of adult learners. This experience facilitated the use of his Canon Communicator. He wrote 'I like my Canon much more now.' At the end of two years he typed a message: 'I have learnt enough for now, thank you.' He had decided that he wanted a break from learning. Two years later on, Stephen's frustration broke out again. He is now on the locked ward of a long-stay hospital. Education offered a means of development and progression before — but it is not available on the locked wards of the hospital.

Claire Bishop lives in a long-stay hospital. In addition to her learning difficulties, she has a visual impairment and a physical disability. She is heavily built, and relies on staff or residents to push her around the hospital in her wheelchair. Claire attends adult education classes at the hospital. She decided to make a record of her life experiences. This was done by means of dictation, some of which was tape-recorded. The finished booklet was published as part of the hospital magazine. It describes Claire's early experiences through to the present day. The text was recorded so that she can listen to her life story whenever she wants. Claire is active in the self advocacy group at the hospital, which is facilitated by an adult education tutor. Claire said: 'We talk about what we would like in the future, and things in general. We learn a bit about the outside world. We've done quite a lot really.' She enjoys discussing issues, and voting on decisions. The hospital's proposed closure has been much discussed. The hospital manager was invited to a meeting to answer questions. The group contacted and interviewed the local MP about the closure, and made a subsequent visit to the Houses of Parliament.

CHANGES IN APPROACH AND LABELS

The recognition of the rights of people with learning difficulties to an ordinary life-style in the community and the chance to pursue socially valued options such as education and work has caused service planners to rethink their provision.

Key words have emerged in health, social services, education and voluntary agencies, to reflect changes in approach.

The concept of *normalisation* or *social role valorisation* underlies many recent developments. Normalisation (sometimes misunderstood as 'trying to make people normal') places emphasis on creating opportunities for people with learning difficulties which are positively valued by others in society. For example, having a job and living in a flat are more highly valued by most people than being unemployed and living on the locked ward of a long-stay hospital.

People with learning difficulties have been socially isolated from the rest of the community in a number of ways, for instance:

- separate, 'special' schools

- separate transport — special buses or ambulances

- long-stay hospitals

- large hostels

- isolated day centres

- special leisure clubs.

They have also been subjected to a variety of 'dehumanising' experiences. Normalisation provides a set of values which help to reverse these negative factors. List A shows a range of dehumanising experiences, while List B shows a complementary range of experiences mediated by normalisation.

Changes in approach and attitude have been reflected in differences in labelling and the development of the self advocacy movement, which is enabling people with learning difficulties to speak up for themselves. The terms once considered acceptable (from 'educationally subnormal' to 'mental handicap') are now

List A	List B
Segregation from others	Opportunities for integration
Low expectations of achievement	High expectations for development
Lack of choice	Provision of individual choice
Being treated childishly	Being treated as an adult and an equal
Denial of rights and dignity	Conferring rights, respect, dignity

increasingly rejected by self advocates and professionals alike in favour of the less stigmatising 'learning difficulties'. It is argued by a few opponents of this move that to discard the label 'mental handicap' will result in a loss of resources for services for people with learning difficulties. However, the change of label to learning difficulties in terms of school education in 1981 did not have this negative effect. Others, resistant to change, say that 'nobody will understand what is meant by learning difficulties.' Increasing usage will bring acceptance and understanding. Avon social services department has requested all staff to use the term learning difficulties, while a recent report on Radio 4's *Today* programme used it in reporting the Carousel Arts Project (see page 84). Another point of view is that changes in terminology empower professionals but not service users or parents. This can be opposed by looking at the views of self advocates, who reject labels such as 'mental handicap'.

The following students' comments reflect on the issues of labelling and being treated as an adult.

> *Talking about 'mental handicap'. Discussion by the 'Talking Together' group.*
>
> *What people have been called*
>
> *Handicapped*
>
> *Mentally handicapped*
>
> *Mental*
>
> *Disabled*
>
> *Backward*
>
> *Subnormal*
>
> *'I've been called all sorts of things, like spastic.'*
>
> *How people with handicaps are treated*
>
> *People in the group thought it was unfair to be called by such names.*
>
> *'I've been called mental. I don't like that. It makes me feel terrible.'*
>
> *People complained of being treated like children rather than adults. One group member had been called a 'baby'.*
>
> *'Some people don't listen to us or take us seriously. It boils me up.'*

> *How people would like to be treated*
>
> *People wanted to be called by their own names rather than by labels.*
>
> *'I would like to be treated as if I'm not handicapped.'*
>
> *'I like to be called by my name.'*
>
> *'I want to be treated like an adult.'*
>
> *'I'm not handicapped. I'd rather be called by my name.'*
>
> *'Other people wouldn't like it if you called them handicapped.'*

THE CAPACITY TO LEARN

People with severe learning difficulties were considered 'ineducable' under the legislation of the 1944 Education Act. In 1971, a major change took place when schools for children with severe learning difficulties were opened as a result of the Education (Handicapped Children) Act of 1970. It is now beyond doubt that people with learning difficulties can learn effectively. Subsequent reports and legislation have reinforced the importance of continuing education for adults with learning difficulties.

Developments in Education for People with Learning Difficulties

1971 Children with severe learning difficulties formerly labelled as 'ineducable' gain the right to school education as the result of the Education (Handicapped Children) Act.

1973 Russell Report states that adult education should be 'readily accessible to all who need it'. This set the agenda for most of the subsequent developmental work in adult education.

1978 Warnock Report highlights the importance of continuing education for adults with learning difficulties.

1979 The Adult and Continuing Education Advisory Council's *A Strategy for the Basic Education of Adults* recommended adult basic education as a national priority.

1981 Act makes assessment of school leavers' needs a statutory requirement. The term learning difficulties is adopted in preference to labels such as 'educationally subnormal' (ESN).

1984 The Further Education Unit's *Learning for Independence* offered an overview of post-16 educational provision at that time for people with severe learning difficulties.

1984 From Coping to Confidence, jointly published by the DES, NFER and FEU, provides a framework for work with young adults with moderate learning difficulties on full-time courses in further education.

1986 Disabled Persons Act.

1988 New Directions (FEU/NFER) provides a curriculum framework for young adults with severe learning difficulties on full-time courses in further education.

1989 DES Circular urges joint working in the field of special educational needs.

1989 Education Reform Act gives special weighting to adult students who have special educational needs and states that 'local authorities shall have regard to the requirements of persons over compulsory school age who have learning difficulties.'

Students with learning difficulties are often only just starting to realise their educational potential when they leave school because learning processes take longer. People without learning difficulties have the option of continuing education to the age of 21 at an institute of higher education. University or polytechnic clearing houses sort applications centrally. For people with learning difficulties, the picture is very different. Although education to 19 is a legal right, some parents still have to struggle.

Post-19, provision is available only on a patchy basis. A few residential colleges offer full-time courses. Most provision is part-time — often for only a couple of hours a week. Some areas have no post-19 provision. There is currently no easy way for parents or students to find out what provision is available, and where. Even when parents spend considerable time and money in telephoning around the country, it is almost impossible to find out about available options.

A PARENT'S PERSPECTIVE

Mrs Howarth is a single parent with an 18-year-old son, Jeffrey. He has moderate learning difficulties arising from brain damage. Between the ages of 8 and 11 he underwent a full-time and rigorous Doman Delcato programme implemented by his mother under supervision from the branch of The British Institute for Brain Damaged Children in Bridgewater, Somerset. Jeffrey had to practise developmental activities, such as crawling, with assistance. He made remarkable strides in his co-ordination and development, and is today a lively teenager who loves playing football. His dream would be to play for Liverpool FC.

Jeffrey went to a secondary school for children with moderate learning difficulties. He continued the Doman Delcato patterning with his mother for three years. Jeffrey then went on a full-time further education course at the local college for one year. At the end of the summer term, his mother was informed that the college would be unable to offer him a second year. Jeffrey was only 17 then, and his mother was aware that he was entitled as a right to full-time education until the age of 19 because of his learning difficulties. His mother describes her feelings: 'I was choked at the thought of education stopping after all this work. Jeffrey is not ready to leave full-time education yet. He's improving steadily every day.'

Mrs Howarth had to fight to obtain a second year at college for Jeffrey. Fortunately she knew what to say — and to whom. Letters to two local Members of Parliament, to the college principal and to a MENCAP education officer achieved the desired effect. Jeffrey was offered a second year at college. However, Mrs Howarth will not be stopping her quest for appropriate full-time further education for Jeffrey. She hopes to find a suitable residential college so that Jeffrey can continue his education once he is 19. She wonders why there is no 'clearing house' system for him as there is for university and polytechnic applicants.

Mrs Howarth worries about how much freedom to give Jeffrey in the inner city area in which they live, and wishes that a support network existed for parents in a similar situation. She regrets that the FE staff do not liaise regularly with parents. She regards this as professionals overlooking a potentially valuable resource. As a teacher herself, Mrs Howarth wonders why her son has never had the chance to learn about: problem solving in maths; a foreign language; music appreciation; science; creative writing; poetry; modern literature; Shakespeare.

The Centre for Studies in Integration in Education (CSIE) has a useful factsheet on the legal right to education for young adults (16—19) with learning difficulties. Available from: CSIE, 4th Floor, 415 Edgeware Road, London NW2 6NB. Tel: 081 452 8642.

Parents as Learners

'I've learnt a lot today. When I go back, I'm going to be a different person.'

The Workers' Educational Association (Western District) held a one day workshop called 'Connect and We

Thrive', aimed at parents of children with special educational needs and at professionals. People talked about ways in which communication between parents and professionals could be improved, and shared information and ideas about support groups and new initiatives, both locally and abroad.

'I'm from a poor background and I thought it was only the elite that could come to things like this and be listened to ... After today I know I can contribute.'

For a workshop report, contact: Mandy Neville, WEA Tutor Organiser, 40 Morse Road, Redfield, Bristol BS5 9LB.

Think for yourself

How broad are the learning options that your provision offers?
Is appropriate full-time education available in your area for people with learning difficulties to the age of 19?
What opportunities does your provision give for relatives to meet for mutual support?
Is there scope for parents to express their own learning needs, and to follow them up?
What resources are allocated for parent education? What opportunities are there for working in partnership with parents, families and carers?
How can relatives and students access post-19 educational opportunities, on a local, regional and national basis?

SIGNIFICANT INEQUALITIES: THE PROJECT FINDINGS

Throughout the information-gathering phase of the NIACE Rowntree project, certain aspects of provision were highlighted which demonstrated stark contrasts.

Geographical Inequalities

Where people with learning difficulties live determines what educational opportunities are available. Inequalities in the geographical distribution of provision were pronounced. In a few areas, people with moderate or severe learning difficulties were able to continue in full-time education to the age of 20 or even 25. In other areas, no full-time provision and only limited part-time opportunities were available post-school. Some people transferred straight from school to a social services day centre at the age of 16 or 19, with no experience or prospect of continuing education in a college or adult education centre. A recent report on day services (*Individuals, Programmes and Plans*) found that 81 per cent of students at social services day centres had no experience of further education.

The resourcing of provision varies significantly. Budgets ranged from a few hundred pounds a year to many thousands of pounds a term. The variations in resourcing were wide. Some areas were only just starting to develop educational provision for adults with learning difficulties. Others had been doing extensive work for some years. The priority the work was given in educational settings seemed to depend on the energy, enthusiasm and initiatives of one or two key people. A range of finance was used, of which a proportion was external to local education authorities (see Chapter 10).

Race, Gender, Age and Disability: Barriers to Learning

A minority of providers made imaginative provision for:

- people with learning difficulties from black and other ethnic minorities

- women with learning difficulties

- students with learning difficulties and additional complications

- older students with learning difficulties.

In general, though, the educational provision offered to these students was extremely limited or even non-existent (see Chapter 10).

Policy

Some providers had extensive policy documents, but little was happening in the field. Other places were involved in high quality work, but had nothing on paper to set out the philosophy, aims and objectives of the service. The disparity was striking. The development of clear policies linked to action plans, with adequate resource allocations, can be an effective step forward. (See also pages 42–4 and 162–3.)

Process and Practice: Central Issues and Dilemmas in Developing Learning Opportunities

The good practice observed during the project incorporated many positive features, to which reference is made throughout the handbook. In summary, the strengths included:

- A student-centred approach, based where possible on negotiated learning, in which students make their own decisions about what they learn and how.

The advantage: Students become empowered by taking control of their own learning. Assessment, goal setting and evaluation can be a shared activity. *The alternative*: Students who are told what to learn, when and how, will become passive rather than active learners. Assessment, goal setting and evaluation are too frequently processes done to rather than with students with learning difficulties.
The difficulties: Students will almost certainly need to learn the skills to communicate and to negotiate. Students who are the loudest may tend to dominate group proceedings. Asking the group to set their own rules may help to resolve this problem.

- An adult approach.

The advantage: Recognising the adult status of students is crucial if they are to be respected and enabled to develop as adult learners. The use of adult materials is essential.

The alternative: The treatment of students as children and the use of pre-school or primary school activities and equipment is entirely inappropriate for adults. Giant sized Lego, coloured cotton reels, nursery friezes with woolly sheep and similar materials should be banned as childish and irrelevant to the learning needs of adults.

The difficulties: Finding appropriate teaching materials at a suitable level. Encouraging attitude change in staff who see adults with learning difficulties as 'boys and girls' — eternal children.

* A wide range of learning options based on student interest and strengths.

The advantage: An approach which builds on strengths and motivation will encourage success in learning. A broad range of learning choices should be open to students with learning difficulties, as it is for students without disabilities.

The alternative: A narrow and exclusive educational focus on literacy and numeracy is common. It is likely to concentrate on the areas where a student has already experienced difficulty. The heavy emphasis often placed on literacy and numeracy for students with learning difficulties may accentuate rather than overcome past failure. This is not to say that literacy/numeracy should never be offered, but that they should be chosen options. The literacy/numeracy focus was based on perceptions of need and linked to the fact that much of the adult education work is carried out by adult basic education tutors.

The difficulty: It is much easier to sit with a group of students in a classroom practising writing (or pre-writing) skills or playing bingo with numbers than to plan imaginative alternatives with students. It can be challenging to construct meaningful contexts to learn reading and writing which draw successfully on the past experience of students.

* The use of real-life materials and situations.

The advantage: Students with learning difficulties learn more easily when learning is based on real-life experience because transfer of learning from artificial teaching situations is limited.

The alternative: Plastic money, 'shopping games', worksheets and other simulations are all of little use to students who will probably not be able to make the conceptual transfer between these 'pretend' situations and real life. One teacher spent a long time drilling holes in pieces of wood in order to teach students how to insert bathroom plugs. He was perplexed when it was suggested that the bathroom itself would be the best place to learn the skill!

The difficulty: Getting out and about to learn skills for independence in context requires additional staffing and resources. Ways forward are offered by the creative use of team tutoring, ancillary help or volunteers.

* Real opportunities for developing self advocacy skills, choices, decision-making and independence.

The advantage: Students become

better able to take control of the direction of their lives, and to participate in planning processes on a personal and political basis.

The alternative: It is easier for staff to make decisions — for example on a trip, deciding where to go, how to get there, what to buy. It is also less productive for the students, especially when the main aim should be to develop learning for personal autonomy.

The difficulty: Students who are shy, institutionalised or withdrawn can take a long time to make decisions. One man working with an artist took six months to select a colour by himself. Students with communication difficulties may need support to find non-verbal ways of communicating their needs and wishes. (See Chapters 2 and 7.)

- Setting learning in a multi-agency framework and working closely with professionals from other agencies.

The advantage: Coherent use can be made of joint planning, resources and strategies. Development plans can be jointly formulated and enacted.

The alternative: Resources, time and effort can be wasted or duplicated if education provision is isolated from other major providers.

The difficulty: Allowing time for liaison work to take place both at tutor and at senior management levels. Double staffing or remission from other duties is required to enable liaison to take place.

- An emphasis on progression.

The advantage: Progression and planning

next steps forward is an important developmental aspect of learning.

The alternative: Getting stuck or trapped in the same situation, perhaps for a number of years. 'I've been at the centre for 15 years now. It's time I did something different. They call it a training centre, but what are they training us for?'

The difficulty: Dependence by students and by staff on a comfortable existing arrangement can be hard to overcome.

- Integration with other adults as equals — whether learning in a classroom or a factory.

The advantage: People with learning difficulties have the right to share ordinary places and activities alongside other people.

The alternative: Segregated provision, which allows little or no mixing with other people in the community.

The difficulty: Successful integration requires support, planning and additional staffing or the use of volunteers. Progress in arranging for integration can be slow.

- A staff support network.

The advantage: Staff need to be well supported and to feel that their work and their students are valued. (See Chapter 10.)

The alternative: Low morale and staff burn out were common complaints from tutors.

The difficulty: Allocating time and resources to facilitate individual, local and regional staff support sessions.

- Establishing and maintaining high quality educational provision.

The alternative: Some providers play 'the numbers game', and opt for quantity rather than quality. Tutors are expected to teach large groups (sometimes as many as 10 or 12 students with severe learning difficulties), or in extremes to 'fiddle' college registers to increase student numbers. Others fail to monitor the quality of educational work taking place.
The difficulty: Persuading managers that numbers of students aren't everything. Finding ways to monitor the quality of teaching.

- The recognition that process is an important aspect of teaching students with learning difficulties.

The alternative: Some managers demand results and end products in order to demonstrate that students with learning difficulties are 'really learning', in terms of concrete, measurable results. This definition of success in terms of objective targets alone is narrow.
The difficulty: Subtle changes in confidence or gradual developments in self advocacy skills cannot be measured on a checklist. Progress is often qualitative rather than quantative. Self esteem, sense of worth, value and personal achievement are aspects of development which are difficult to measure but vital.

SUMMARY AND SUGGESTIONS FOR ACTION

The development of high quality learning opportunities for adults with learning difficulties must clearly take a range of issues on board.

The NIACE Rowntree project collected details from practitioners across agencies and drew from a representative sample of work to illustrate the themes that emerged. A range of learning difficulty, learning activity, agency and geographical location was used to determine the project visits.

Progress has been made in some places, but the availability and quality of provision fluctuates from one geographical area to another. A national policy is urgently needed, and detailed recommendations are made at the end of each chapter on specific areas of provision.

From the information gathered for the NIACE Rowntree Project, it is evident that there is scope for development in the following broad areas:

- Developing policy statements on adult continuing education for people with learning difficulties, which are linked to clear action plans and set in a multidisciplinary context.

- Examining ways of securing resources to develop provision.

- Creating jointly owned staff development opportunities on a multi-agency basis.

- Developing various means of educating the wider community in order to develop positive attitudes towards people with learning difficulties.

Specific issues related to provision include:

- Extending the curriculum to offer a full range of learning opportunities.

- Developing student-centred approaches to learning involving negotiation rather than 'slotting' people into ready-made courses.

- Using clear assessment, planning, recording and evaluation techniques which involve the student as much as possible.

- Liaising effectively both within organisations and across agencies to ensure continuity.

- Offering increased opportunities for participation in integrated settings.

- Developing appropriate educational programmes for adults with learning difficulties who have additional complications.

- Responding to equal opportunities issues with regard to race and gender in the design and evaluation of provision.

- Facilitating the use of adult, age appropriate materials and activities.

FURTHER READING AND RESOURCES

Living Like Other People. Independent Development Council, 1985.

Adults with Special Needs: A curriculum perspective. Further Education Unit, 1987.

John O'Brien & Alan Tyne *The Principle of Normalisation: A foundation for effective services*. Values into Action, 1981.

Hilary Brown & Jan Alcoe *New Lifestyles for People with Learning Difficulties: A training exercise for staff based on the principle of normalisation*. Pavilion Publishing, 1988.

A staff development pack on values/ attitudes/normalisation is available from PLAN Publications, PO Box 1352, Alvechurch, Worcs.

Think for yourself

What learning opportunities for adults with learning difficulties are available in your local area?
How can staff across agencies work together to improve learning opportunities?
What are the strengths of current provision?
Where are the gaps? How can the range and quality of learning be developed?
Who would need to be involved to effect change?
What are the staff development needs?

Problems
with boy and
girlfriends

oney

arguments

2. Self advocacy and citizen advocacy

Self advocacy: *'Self advocacy is the act of making choices and decisions and bringing about desired change for oneself ... Any activity that involves self determination can be called self advocacy.'* (The Growing Voice, Bronach Crawley.)

Citizen advocacy: *'Citizen Advocate: A competent, unpaid citizen volunteer with minimal conflict of interest ... who relates to, and/or represents and advocates for, the interests and needs of a person in need.'* (PASSING, Wolf Wolfensberger and Susan Thomas.)

SELF ADVOCACY

'It's only fair that people should learn to speak up.' (Self advocate.)

Self advocacy is commonly described as people with learning difficulties 'speaking up' or 'speaking out' for themselves. Self-expression is an important aspect of self advocacy, but change is the feature which distinguishes self advocacy from learning to express oneself.

From the information gathered for the NIACE Rowntree Project, relatively few providers state that learning about self advocacy is offered as part of their educational provision. Only 15 out of 315 places mentioned self advocacy when outlining their learning opportunities for the project. In an informal survey by Andrea Whittaker at the King's Fund Centre, only 5 out of 64 self advocacy groups were based in an adult or further education setting. This is a matter of some concern. Self advocacy should be a key component of learning, underpinning the development of a curriculum built on student choice, decision-making and empowerment.

The implementation of the Disabled Persons Act (1986) will require people with learning difficulties to be more actively involved in planning their futures. The White Paper *Caring for People* (1989) states that the provision of community care services to people with learning difficulties should be made with 'proper participation of the individuals concerned'. The development of self advocacy skills will be crucial to support these initiatives.

This chapter highlights a number of different aspects of self advocacy under the following headings:

- Self advocacy and individual change

- Organising learning in a framework of self advocacy

- Recognising life stories and experiences

- Developing black self advocacy

- Learning about self advocacy

- Independent self advocacy groups

- Self advocates as tutors and planners

- Staff development

- Self advocacy without words

- Self advocacy for people who have been institutionalised.

SELF ADVOCACY AND INDIVIDUAL CHANGE

In personal terms, the development of choices and decisions by students with learning difficulties about their lives can take place on a variety of levels. Day-to-day decisions, such as selecting what to wear or what to eat, are often new and difficult for people unused to personal autonomy. With time and encouragement, people gain confidence in making choices. The level and complexity of decision-making and independence can be increased. Decisions which affect the course of one's life — such as deciding to get a job, to leave home or to get married — are choices which have been made by people with learning difficulties advocating for themselves. These decisions can be challenging for parents and professionals, whose desire to protect and safeguard can lead them to take decision-making away from people with learning difficulties.

Think for yourself

List all the choices and decisions you have made in the last two days in everyday matters (what to wear, what time to go to bed).
List personal decisions that have affected your life in major ways. Think about or talk to a student that you know well in relation to the above issues. How do his or her opportunities to make choices and decisions compare to yours, both in everyday matters and in major decisions?

ORGANISING LEARNING IN A FRAMEWORK OF SELF ADVOCACY: ACHIEVING INSTITUTIONAL CHANGE

Learning should offer maximum opportunities for students to plan for themselves and to make choices and decisions. This has implications for the way that learning is structured and organised within an institution. A framework of self advocacy can be developed by:

- Empowering students to take control of their learning by adopting a student-centred approach. At Northumberland College, students with learning difficulties decide what directions they would like their lives to go in and what they would like to achieve. Objectives and goals are set by students themselves.

- Enabling students to experience choice and decision-making. At Newcastle College, students with moderate learning difficulties make up their own timetables from a wide range of courses.

- Providing opportunities for students to be involved in planning for themselves. At Streatham and Tooting Adult Education Institute, students with learning difficulties run a committee which comments on the educational provision. Bids can be put in for new courses.

These three themes are at the heart of developing good practice through a student-centred approach, and will recur throughout the handbook, illustrated in a variety of ways.

Think for yourself

How can all learning programmes be developed to give greater opportunities for:
student empowerment?
choice?
decision-making?
involvement in planning processes?

RECOGNISING LIFE STORIES AND EXPERIENCES

'You must begin to tell your stories — tell people what has happened to you.' (Self advocate.)

The recognition of past experience enhances the sense of self-image and self-esteem for all of us. Educational settings offer a positive atmosphere for people with learning difficulties to reminisce, recollect and value past experience, which is a valid part of the development of self advocacy skills.

At Streatham and Tooting Adult Education Institute, women of a variety of ages and backgrounds have spent time sharing and documenting their past and present experiences. The lack of opportunity and choice still facing many people with learning difficulties is clearly expressed in the following account, as is the richness of interests of the student:

'I was born in Romania, in a German hospital in 1940 in the middle of the war. When I was six months I travelled by sea all the way round Africa and back to Britain. I am now 49. I have been at St Michael's Convent for 29 years. I like going to the theatre and the cinema. I like to see Shakespearean plays and I love Italian food. Nobody explained to me why I had to go to a convent. I just had to go like that. I had no choice. It still makes me very sad and upset. At the convent we have to get up too early and go to bed about 8 o'clock. I never get a chance to watch the news on television.' (Jocelyn Thomson.)

In the following account, handling racial prejudice and longing for a former home in Africa are both poignant themes.

*'I had an accident when I was a little girl in my country. I went to hospital. I'm from Somalia in Africa. It's very hot there, you can just wear T-shirts most of the time. We had a big house in Somalia. I'd like to go back and stay with my gran; I miss her very much. I like Somalian food, it's very different to what I get at the convent where I live. It's spicy food.
I was a twin, my twin died. I didn't know 'cause I was at school and when my brother told me I was very upset and locked myself in my room. My mum moved to London, the rest of my family are in Somalia.
My social worker took me to the convent. I didn't like it because people call me names like Blackie.*

They shouldn't do that. Also I'm Muslim and they tell me to eat bacon.
I used to work at Lingfield Hospital, making the beds. It was nice there, I like to work. I had to stop work when I went to the convent. I miss it, but most of all I'd like to go back to Africa.' (Zenab Omar.)

Lastly, to demonstrate that age is not a barrier to development, older women describe their lives.

'I used to live in Darenth Park before it closed. I used to work there. I liked it, I'd clean the nurses' bikes. I love Our Lady, I'd like to live at the convent, I'd like to go to Mass everyday. Jesus gave me a good life, I'm looking forward to going "up there". In 1990 I'll be getting a telegram and boy oh boy what a party. There have been so many changes in my life. The shops are so big now. I remember the little old shops. You could get toffee, cake and broken up biscuits, it's all much more expensive now.'(Alice, 98 years old.)

'I am 84 years old, I remember both the wars, they were terrible. You couldn't go out and life was very dull. My mother was French, she was lovely. I remember her cooking. We had an orchard when I was young, we would have picnics. She made jams and pies from the blackberries. After my mother died, my father said he thought it would be best for me to go to the convent, so I am here at St

Michael's now. I used to work in the laundry but I'm too old for that now.' (Marie-Rose.)

The women speaking were all part of the same adult education group. The group gave positive recognition to the experiences of all of the women involved. Age and race presented no object to participation in this example of good practice, which was rare. A women-only group was also unusual. Recognising the fact that women may find it harder to speak up, Westminster People First planned assertiveness training courses for women only. Newham Community College has provided a 'Self Preservation' course for women with learning difficulties, which offers a mixture of assertiveness, self advocacy and self defence.

Think for yourself

Dictating or writing life stories, collecting/taking photographs, painting, poetry and using tape recorders/video offer a few ways of recording experience.
What opportunities could be developed locally for people with learning difficulties to describe and value their life experiences? How can self advocacy provision be established to cater particularly for the needs of:
* *students from black and other ethnic minority groups?*
* *women?*
* *older adults?*
* *younger adults aged 16—19?*

DEVELOPING BLACK SELF ADVOCACY

'White people think black people and Indian people come to this country and cause violence. They blame them.'
'When we go out white people stare at us.'
'Whether you are black or white, you are your own person and you should be proud of yourself. Just because some few people discriminate against other races you should not let yourself down.'

These are comments made by black people with learning difficulties who attended a meeting called 'Sharing Experiences' in Brixton. The meeting was a spin off from a project which aimed to develop training materials on anti-racist practice in work with people who have learning difficulties. The project was a joint venture between the London Boroughs Training Committee (LBTC) and the Central Council on Education and Training in Social Work (CCETSW).

Peter Ferns, Training and Development Manager (LBTC), describes the 'Sharing Experiences' meeting:

'Black people with learning difficulties are caught in the intersection of two great oppressions in society, racism and discrimination against people with disabilities. The oppressive experiences of some black people with learning difficulties makes it even more impressive that so many people have come through the experience with dignity and strength. We met some of these people at the meeting. We also met people who were lacking in self-confidence, angry and frustrated with the services they receive, isolated and lonely but eager to communicate with each other and express their life experiences. There was something special about that day because the confidence and trust of some people visibly grew as black people relaxed and talked in small groups with other black people. There was a common language, people knew and fully understood the experience of being racially abused and discriminated against in housing and jobs. There was no need to justify, be apologetic or provide evidence. There was also a sharing of good things such as happy experiences of family life, the achievements of some people in finding jobs and somewhere to live.'

Peter found that many of the group wanted to meet again, preferably on a regular basis. From this interest grew the idea of developing black self advocacy groups. One group has been established in Hackney. Approximately 12 self advocates meet every two or three weeks. Peter facilitates the group, and finds his social work experience of group work to be valuable. On some occasions, the group has met without him.

Another group is planned for Brixton. To date no funding is available for development work and Peter Ferns is already working in his own time. He is anxious that the Hackney group develops an identity gradually, and feels that too much publicity could be damaging. He is currently trying to generate interest and contacts. He says: 'Black self advocacy should be on the agenda.'

Think for yourself

How can black self advocacy groups be established?
What resources would be needed?
How can black self advocacy groups link in to wider self advocacy initiatives?
How can black women with learning difficulties participate fully in self advocacy?

LEARNING ABOUT SELF ADVOCACY

'I have had a few thoughts about what sort of courses in self advocacy could be taught. I think that it is important to have courses for beginners in self advocacy, for people who have had little or no experience in speaking up. Then to have separate courses for people who are more advanced, once people get used to speaking up for themselves in meetings, etc. I also think that it would be a good idea to have self advocacy courses for the general public, where people could learn about self advocacy, and could come to have a greater understanding of people with disabilities.' (Gary Bourlet, President, People First, London and Thames.)

Many practitioners acknowledge that self advocacy is 'something they ought to be doing'. Getting started is hard. This section looks at the benefits in developing specific courses on the theme of self advocacy and at the skills which can be developed. It looks briefly at some materials, and profiles one group's development.

Self Advocacy Courses

Specific courses offer an effective way of developing self advocacy. The City Lit in London has offered classes to adults with learning difficulties since 1979. The learning opportunities all offer possibilities for development and self-expression, for example through story telling, dance, music and art. 'A Chance to Speak' and 'Speaking for Ourselves' and other classes offer a 'talking shop' for people with learning difficulties to gain confidence in speaking up for themselves. Creating time and space for talking is essential, according to tutor John Hersov. Former students have become actively involved in independent self advocacy groups.

Education should offer courses with the aim of developing self advocacy, to include learning to:

- listen to other people

- speak up for oneself and others

- be in a group

- ask and to answer questions

- take turns in speaking

- communicate effectively

- value opinions and experience

- be assertive, and to understand the difference between assertion and aggression

- express views

- recognise citizens' rights

- offer support to others

- use body language to support communication

- make choices and decisions

- plan for change: whether individual or collective.

Self Advocates on Self Advocacy

'At first I found self advocacy a bit hard to learn. I couldn't speak up for myself. Now I can do whatever I want to do. It has changed me a lot. I can speak up for myself.'

'It's helped a lot. I help my friends and other people to speak up and not to be frightened.'

'It's got a long way to go. People outside have got to realise that this is what people want.'

'Self advocacy is talking for yourself — going to meetings — not being dependent on other people to speak for you.'

'If you don't speak up, you keep silent. That's not good.'

'This class is very worthwhile. There's a lot of things I can't talk about anywhere else that I can talk about here, because there's less pressure. I've got a more grown up attitude since coming here.'

(Comments from members of the London MENCAP/Participation Forum, and from students at the City Lit, London.)

Learning about skills for meetings is another valid role for education, which can incorporate:

- learning the language of meetings, to include the meanings of words like 'agenda', 'minutes,' 'apologies'

- learning about the format and structure of meetings

- devising a set of rules for meetings such as 'no smoking', 'only one person at a time to speak'

- learning the roles of different people at meetings — chairperson, secretary.

A Profile of a Self Advocacy Group in Adult Education

'People should listen to what we have to say.'

'The group gives us freedom to have our own say.'

The 'Talking Together' group started meeting in November 1987. It meets once a month on Saturday mornings at an adult education centre in Luton. The meeting used to last for an hour and a half, but students voted to extend the time to two hours. Twelve students attend regularly. The majority of the group live at home with parents. Some live in a social services hostel and one person lives independently. One person has a job — the others attend the four day centres in the area. The mixture of backgrounds has been a positive shaping force, as students have compared their various experiences. From the outset, the students have chosen the topics for discussion. These have included:

- the future of centres

- labelling

- where people would like to live

- the closure of the local long-stay hospital for people with learning difficulties

- work

- wages

- friends.

The group is facilitated by two adult education tutors. This has been helpful, as the tutors have been able to monitor each other's levels of participation to ensure that the group is student-led and not tutor-dominated. Changes in the balance of the group have occurred over the three years. At first, students required encouragement to speak, and tutors took this prompting role. Students gradually became more spontaneous in group discussion. After 12 sessions, students started to chair the meetings for themselves. They decided on a rota for this responsibility. The tutors take a back seat and offer support when needed. The group's achievements include:

- running a training day for local professionals in collaboration with 'People First' of London

- presenting an input to 75 librarians on a staff training day

- calling a meeting and inviting social services managers to come and answer questions about day centre provision

- participating in a user forum.

Outside support has been obtained by tutors and students attending three training events held by the King's Fund Centre and by Skill, the National Bureau for Students with Disabilities.

A current goal is to obtain air space on local radio in order to 'explain to the public about our group'.

Students who have been involved in self advocacy work in adult education settings have as a result felt more confident both in everyday and in public situations. The developing confidence and assertiveness carries over from the self advocacy groups into everyday life.

'I don't know what you've been doing with Ronnie, but he stood up and gave a marvellous speech at a leaving party. I didn't know he was capable of this!' (Nurse at a long-stay hospital.)

'I went into my case conference and I told them straight what I wanted. I said to them — I can say what I want to say now, and it's all thanks to the "Talking Together" group.' (Adult education student.)

'Thanks for all you've done with Mark. He's so confident now, in all kinds of situations.' (Parent.)

Think for yourself

Does local provision offer specific courses in developing self advocacy and skills for meetings?
If not, how could such courses become established?

ACHIEVING WIDER CHANGE THROUGH INDEPENDENT SELF ADVOCACY GROUPS

There is a tension in that for self advocacy to provide an independent voice, self advocacy groups should be independent of services. Although services can help to foster skills for self advocacy and skills for meetings, self advocacy groups cannot be independent if they are staffed by people whose loyalties are split between the students they work with and the establishment they work for. There are ways to overcome this. For example, 'People First' of London has obtained external funding to employ staff; 'Skills for People' in Newcastle is a registered charity, which seeks funding from a variety of sources.

Achievements by groups of self advocates have included:

- securing voting rights for residents in a long-stay hospital

- persuading London Transport to remove 'H' for 'Handicapped' from concessionary bus passes

- successful campaigns to remove stigmatising labels from minibuses and from buildings

- participating in interviews for day centre staff.

Self advocacy is clearly a political as well as a personal issue.

Think for yourself

Is there an independent self advocacy group in the area?
If not, could one be facilitated with independent advisers?
How would it be funded and supported?

SELF ADVOCATES AS TUTORS AND PLANNERS

Self Advocates as Tutors

'Skills for People' in Newcastle upon Tyne is a registered charity which offers opportunities for people with disabilities (learning difficulties, physical disabilities, sensory impairment) to design and tutor courses for people with disabilities and for professionals. The project is the only one of its kind in the UK, and is based on the philosophy that 'all people have a right to decide for themselves how to live their lives'. Courses have been run in a variety of settings, including long-stay hospitals and hostels. Topics have included:

- making friends

- self advocacy and speaking up for yourself

- planning for yourself — your life and future

- lifestyles

- living independently in the community

- attitudes of people in the community
- welfare rights
- relationships and sexuality.

Three paid staff members support and advise the students. Progress can be slow, especially for people new to planning, organising and speaking up for themselves. On the other hand, some students are now so confident that they travel long distances to give inputs at conferences by themselves. The work is funded by a mixture of grants from social services, local authorities and charitable trusts. Transport is a major cost, as many students cannot travel independently.

An evaluation report highlights the strengths of 'Skills for People':

'The primary way in which the project helps disabled people to develop self-confidence is to involve them as members of teams which plan, teach and evaluate various short courses about issues which affect their everyday lives. This gives people a chance to make real decisions; discussed according to what they want rather than what others suggest is good for them. They learn to take control over their lives through the experience of having control over a workshop — where it will be held, when, how long, what topics will be discussed, who will make the presentations and who will be invited to attend. The focus of attention is on what people can do, which leads to increased self-confidence and less dependence on others.'

Think for yourself

How can self advocates be enabled to design and run courses?
What support and resources would be necessary?

Self Advocates as Planners

Given the chance, people with learning difficulties can plan and organise conferences. In September 1988, the 'People First' group hosted an international conference on self advocacy in London.

Groups of self advocates from various places have organised conferences on the theme of self advocacy. The 1990 UK 'People First' conference was planned by a number of groups from around the country.

Many providers aim to involve users with learning difficulties in planning and developing services. This laudable intention is often unrealised, as in the case of user groups which comprise mainly parents rather than service users with learning difficulties. There are challenges which must be overcome to realise the full participation of people with learning difficulties in planning processes. People with learning difficulties have been invited to join in formal planning meetings, where the professional language used and the levels of literacy required to understand minutes and agenda present blocks to participation. There is a clear tutorial role both in preparing self advocates to understand the details and processes of such meetings and in supporting self advocates to gain confidence in voicing their opinions during meetings.

People committed to change are starting to find ways of involving people with learning difficulties in order to learn from their experiences. Hillingdon Social Services and the North West Thames Regional Health Authority are consulting with members of 'People First' about setting up group homes. 'People First' members have been able to advise the professionals about issues which are important to residents of group homes, such as privacy, and having a personal key.

In South Bedfordshire, the User Forum is attended by two self advocates from a local group. They are supported by an adviser who can interpret the minutes, agenda and any 'technical language'. The self advocates have commented on topics such as housing and labelling. Minutes from the meetings are considered directly by senior managers of services.

Think for yourself

What opportunities can be developed for students to become actively involved in planning services? How can full participation in planning be realised, as opposed to tokenism?

STAFF DEVELOPMENT

'It can all go too far, you know this self advocacy business. It could get out of hand.' (Day centre manager.)

There are still fears and misconceptions about the nature of self advocacy. These are just some of the anxieties which have been expressed:

- staff believe self advocacy to be subversive or militant

- staff fear losing control

- tutors see self advocacy as a threat to the 'known and safe' curriculum

- parents feel undermined when their sons/daughters assert themselves, or worry when risk-taking is a possibility

- staff believe that self advocacy leads to people with learning difficulties developing unrealistic expectations.

These fears are most frequently expressed by people who are viewing self advocacy cynically and at a distance, rather than seeing what the benefits and strengths are at first hand. People without learning difficulties have every right to make choices and decisions and to change their lives in any way they legally can. Self advocacy gives people with learning difficulties the opportunity to enjoy the same citizens' rights. Some people find this shift in the balance of power disturbing and threatening. It challenges assumptions and roles.

Staff development is an essential aspect of self advocacy. *We Can Change the Future* by John Hersov and Deborah Cooper is an invaluable book and video resource pack aimed at professionals, which covers self advocacy in greater depth than is possible here, with information and exercises for staff. (For details, see the resources section.)

South Glamorgan has developed a local training scheme, which has led to new provision being set up. South Glamorgan Community Education Service, in co-operation with South Glamorgan Institute of Higher Education, has run annual short courses since 1987 to train tutors in the development of self-advocacy skills. Self advocates have presented part of these courses. Seven self advocacy groups are meeting in Community Education Centres throughout the county, led by tutors who have completed the training course. In total 62 students attend, and transport is provided for most of them. The courses were advertised in general adult education prospectuses. Classes are supported by a part-time co-ordinator who is responsible for development and evaluation of provision, publicity, applications and transport organisation. The work is jointly funded by education and social services. Tutors meet together for mutual support and curriculum development. A meeting for parents and support workers was held to explain likely changes in the students in order that carers will support and reinforce the move towards independence. Further work in this area is desirable. Students, parents/carers and community education officers were sent questionnaires in order to discover their views on the courses. Students are enthusiastic about the courses and good progress is being made.

Self Advocates as Staff Trainers

Some self advocacy groups or students provide inputs at staff training events. It makes clear sense for people with learning

difficulties to talk about self advocacy, rather than for professionals to speak on their behalf. This arrangement also challenges the assumptions and prejudices that staff may have, when for a change they are on the receiving end of inputs from students with learning difficulties.

Think for yourself

What staff development opportunities are available both locally and nationally for tutors to learn about self advocacy?
How can self advocates become more involved in providing staff development on self advocacy?

SELF ADVOCACY WITHOUT WORDS

For people who are unable to communicate verbally, the development of self advocacy skills will depend on the appropriate method of alternative communication. By sign, symbol, gesture, eye pointing or other means students can learn to choose between alternatives and to make their needs and wishes known. Learning to use a computer switch to signal 'yes' or 'no' can be the beginning of a process of self determination. (See the section on communication in Chapter 7.)

Students unable to speak can still make their learning preferences known. At Pewsey Hospital, students attending the Wyvern Special Education Centre are encouraged to choose their own learning activities. Students without speech who can recognise photographs are encouraged to look at a row of photos which show various activities/items around the room, ranging from the computer to the biscuits. The students can then point at a photo to indicate their choice. For extra durability the photos are individually mounted on special wooden backings (made by students at the centre) and are also laminated. The Makaton symbol for each item is shown on the back of each photograph. This is useful for students who can use the symbols alone, as well as for students who are learning to associate the symbol with the object.

Think for yourself

How can students without speech make their needs and wishes known? How can students without speech be included in self advocacy courses/ groups?

SELF ADVOCACY WITH INSTITUTIONALISED STUDENTS

People who have spent time in long-stay hospitals and who are institutionalised may need extra time and support in starting to develop self advocacy. Certain skills may need to be slowly acquired, such as learning to be part of a group, to take turns and to listen. Moving out to live in the community will offer greater choices for decision-making and communication:

'*After six months, Dennis has learnt to choose his own food and what to wear.*

Last week he said "no" for the first time!' (Adult education tutor.)

Organising self advocacy work within a long-stay hospital can create tensions if other staff are not supportive:

'*I used to worry that I was encouraging the students to speak up and to value their views, when in fact the more assertive residents seemed to be the ones who got into trouble with some of the nurses.*' (Adult education tutor.)

Think for yourself

Is there a local long-stay hospital for people with learning difficulties? If so, is self advocacy work taking place there? If not, who could facilitate a group? How can people resident in a hospital participate in a community-based self advocacy group?

CITIZEN ADVOCACY AND LEARNING

The relationship between citizen advocacy and learning has yet to be fully explored but offers exciting possibilities.

Citizen advocates befriend and represent individuals with very severe learning difficulties who are unable to advocate effectively for themselves, for example at individual planning meetings. The implementation of the Disabled Persons Act (1986) will mean a growth in the use of volunteer citizen advocates to protect the interests and rights of people with severe disabilities.

Jennie Ephgrave is developing the Vale

and South Oxon Citizen Advocacy scheme. She describes the actual and potential contribution of citizen advocates in her area to the learning process:

'One citizen advocate is playing a part in extending the independence skills of her partner by talking about menus and prices, and going supermarket shopping together. This ties in with the staff-run programme to teach sufficient cooking skills for the resident to manage main meals with her flat mate and thus become truly independent from the main establishment.

I would most certainly expect that advocates would be looking at learning possibilities for their partners. In fact my main hope for two quite profoundly handicapped women in their early twenties is that the involvement of citizen advocates on their behalf will succeed in helping to negotiate special learning programmes for them. Another partner would like a real job in catering, but was not accepted by the local college catering course as they felt he would not cope with the academic aspects. Perhaps his advocate (and I think I have found one for him) will explore other ways of getting appropriate training to achieve his ambition. Of course, just going out and about with their advocate, seeing new places and meeting new people, is a learning experience in itself.'

Kathy West describes the contribution of citizen advocates working for the

Camberwell Citizen Advocacy office:

'Camberwell advocates have made an enormous contribution to the lives of many local adults with learning difficulties in the informal sense. That has ranged from encouraging their partners to try new experiences, helping them learn new skills and polish up existing ones while being generally supportive towards achieving greater opportunities. Bryan, for example, has encouraged his partner to become a better swimmer and is teaching him to type. Hilary is going new places with her partner, and a few weeks ago her partner successfully used an escalator for the first time. Jane has taught John a lot about friendship (he hadn't had a friend before), family life and what people do in social situations.'

Think for yourself

How can citizen advocacy schemes be developed and funded?
How can citizen advocates contribute to the process of negotiating or facilitating learning for students unable to advocate for themselves?

RECOMMENDATIONS

- 1. A Student-centred Approach

A student-centred approach should be adopted which enables students to take control of their own learning.

Opportunities for choice and decision making should be offered in all learning activities.
Students should be involved in planning for themselves.

- 2. Self Advocacy

Specific courses on the development of self advocacy should be offered in all learning programmes.
Sensitive ways of informing parents and support workers about the goals of self advocacy must be developed if students are to become more autonomous in their home settings. Self advocates should be actively involved in staff development and training.

- 3. Citizen Advocacy

The role of citizen advocacy in learning is as yet under-developed, but offers exciting possibilities. Ways must be found of involving citizen advocates in negotiating or facilitating learning.

FURTHER READING AND RESOURCES

Materials for Developing Self Advocacy

Learning About Self Advocacy. Values into Action, 1988.
This pack is aimed at students with learning difficulties. It consists of five A4 booklets on different themes: What is self advocacy? Getting going; Running a group; What next? Basic skills that help. It has large print and line drawings, but manages to be adult in appearance. It is designed as a self-help pack. People without literacy skills will need support to work their way through it. Available from: Values into Action, 5 Kentings, Comberton, Cambs CB3 7DT.

Working Together. Open University course P555(M). This is an adaptation of the *Patterns for Living* pack, which has been designed for students with learning difficulties. Materials are presented on audiotape, video and in an illustrated workbook. Concepts such as self advocacy, normalisation and integration are clearly presented. Individual study packs or group study packs are available with notes for guidance. For further information contact: Jennifer Rook, Department of Health and Social Welfare, The Open University, Walton Hall, Milton Keynes MK7 6AA. Tel: 0908 653743.

Hilary Brown *Whose Lifestyle? A package to enable people with learning difficulties to speak for themselves*. Pavilion Publishing, 1988.
This pack contains 60 black and white photographs showing a range of situations relating to social options and lifestyles. It aims to enable people with learning difficulties to express preferences and to make choices about their own lives — from where to live to having a job. It is suggested that the materials are used in three consecutive stages to support people with learning difficulties in: expressing preferences; reviewing services; making changes.

Resources for Self Advocacy

John Hersov & Deborah Cooper *We Can Change the Future*. Skill (National Bureau for Students with Disabilites), 1986.

Paul Williams & Bonnie Shoultz *We Can Speak For Ourselves*. Souvenir Press, 1982.

Bronach Crawley *The Growing Voice*. Values Into Action, 1988.

Alison Wertheimer *Self Advocacy and Parents. The impact of advocacy on the parents of young people with disabilities*. Further Education Unit, 1989.

Mariette Clare *Developing Self Advocacy Skills*. Further Education Unit/REPLAN, 1990.

Writing by People with Learning Difficulties

Julie Ward (ed.) *Secret Lives*. Yorkshire Art Circus and Swarthmore Education Centre, 1989.

Edie Wildey *My Life Story*. Skill (National Bureau for Students with Disabilities), 1987.

Play Back the Thinking Memories. National Children's Bureau, 1987.

Dorothy Atkinson & Fiona Williams (eds) *Know Me As I Am. An anthology of prose, poetry and art by people with learning difficulties*. Hodder & Stoughton, 1990. 'Changing Perspectives' (Open University course K668), aimed at professionals, centres on *Know Me As I Am*,

which comprises the work of people with learning difficulties.

Selected resources have been listed. Full listings of resources on self advocacy are available from: Andrea Whittaker, King's Fund Centre, 126 Albert Street, London NW1 7NF. Andrea is also building a self advocacy network and is pleased to share details and information.

For printed materials, a reading list is available from: Values Into Action (Formerly CMH), Oxford House, Derbyshire Street, London E2 6HG.

Addresses

The national self advocacy network is: People First, People First Office, Oxford House, Derbyshire Street, London E2 6HG (tel: 071 739 3890). The national citizen advocacy group is: National Citizen Advocacy Resource and Advisory Centre, 2 St Paul's Road, London N1 2QR.

Skills for People, Haldane House, Tankerville Terrace, Jesmond Newcastle upon Tyne NE2 3AH.

SITE (Section for Independence through Education), The City Lit, Stukely Street, Drury Lane, London WC2B 5LJ.

An independent self advocacy consultant is John Hersov, 23 Willoughby Road, Hampstead, London NW3 1RT.

Details of black self advocacy groups from: Peter Ferns, Training and Development Manger, London Boroughs Training Committee, 9 Tavistock Place, London WC1H 9SN.

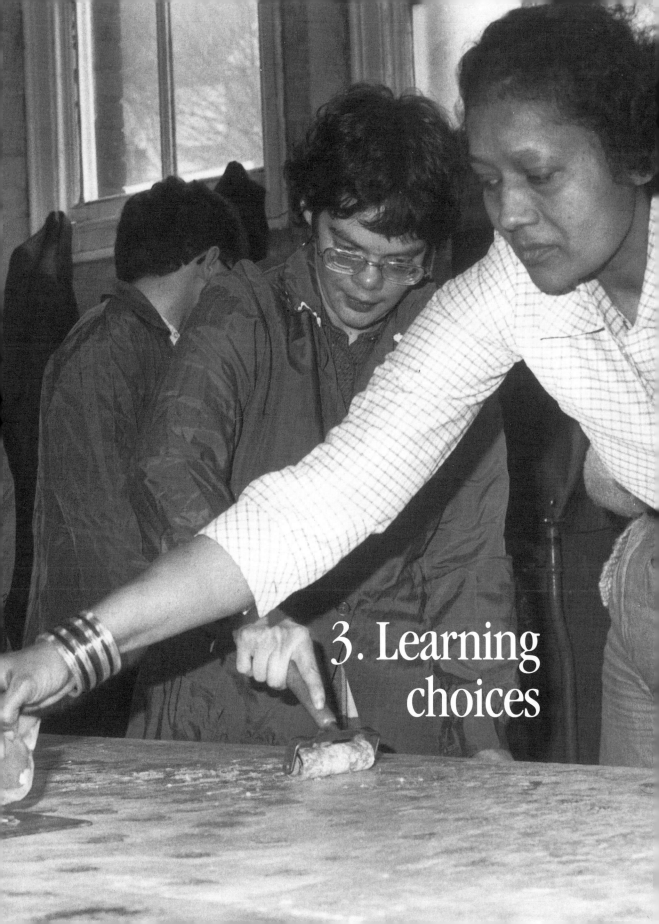

3. Learning
choices

WHO DECIDES WHO SHOULD LEARN — AND WHAT?

For adults, learning is usually a freely-chosen voluntary activity. People choose to learn for a variety of reasons, including:

- development of skills related to employment

- studying for a qualification

- self-development through learning a new skill

- learning for pleasure and fun.

Adults with learning difficulties have often been distanced from the processes of choice and decision-making on the question of whether, and what, to learn. Skills for independence have sometimes been emphasised to the exclusion of other learning activities. People can be sentenced to a lifetime of learning, without having any say in the matter. The following examples are all taken from real life situations:

- students have been sent to education classes 'because it will be good for them'

- the same day centre students attend college each year 'because their names are on the list'

- students have been bussed in from the local day centre to learn engineering 'because the engineering lecturer had a space in his timetable for a few weeks'. In one hospital, large groups of residents are sent to evening classes *en bloc*. The wards are locked, giving the residents no choice of opting out and returning home.

These arrangements are not responsive to student interests and motivation, but are based instead on staff convenience. Students with learning difficulties have often received restricted and unimaginative teaching, often characterised by:

- pre-school or primary school-type activities and materials, which are inappropriate for adults

- students timetabled in to learn subjects which may not be of interest or relevance

- limited opportunities, in that often only skills for independence are taught. Some providers offer *only* literacy and numeracy to students with learning difficulties — yet these are the subjects they are most likely to have already experienced failure in

- limited choice, in that it is frequently staff and not students who make decisions about who should have the chance to learn — and what.

OPENING UP NEW OPPORTUNITIES

In order to develop a student-centred approach, the following key questions must be addressed:

- How can students gain access to information about what learning opportunities are available?

- How can students make informed decisions about what to learn?

- How can students influence the range of learning options available? What are the organisational issues in using available resources flexibly to support a student-centred approach?

- How can agencies collaborate to ensure that provision is coherently planned?

ACCESS TO INFORMATION ABOUT LEARNING OPPORTUNITIES

Most adults contemplating a course of study will browse through several prospectuses, looking for something of interest or relevance to them. A further education college or adult education centre prospectus usually relies on the printed word to explain what is on offer. Publicity about opportunities for students with learning difficulties should be available in all college and adult education centre brochures, prospectuses and advertisements. Clear statements should be included which cite equal opportunities policies and welcome applications from students with disabilities for all courses. Some students with learning difficulties may have difficulty in reading, but their friends, families and support workers — as well as the general public — need to know that learning opportunities are available for people with learning difficulties. Students with learning difficulties should have the right to enjoy the full curriculum range of subjects open to all adult learners. An example of this sort of welcoming publicity from a

general prospectus published by South Glamorgan Community Education Service is shown on page 38.

As many people with learning difficulties have limited reading skills, they are often denied the chance to find out what learning activities are being offered at an education centre. Other ways must be found to explain the available options.

Alternatives to the Written Prospectus

Photographic and Pictorial Prospectuses. Photographs, slides or illustrations can usefully present a visual image of some subject areas. Students can browse through and find a subject they would like to try. Visual images must be clear and unambiguous. Subjects which are activity-based (for example woodwork or yoga) translate clearly to a visual image. However, photographs of groups based on communication and discussion (for example French or self advocacy) or on written work (English, maths) are hard to distinguish from one another.

One adult education team provides several photographs and a brief description of each learning activity on offer. These are displayed on the main notice boards in the local social services day centres for several weeks before the start of the academic year. Students can choose which subjects they are interested in, and can discuss the matter with their keyworker if they choose to. The students can sign their name by their chosen options. If they are unable to write their name, a friend or keyworker can help.

OPPORTUNITIES FOR ADULTS WITH SPECIAL NEEDS

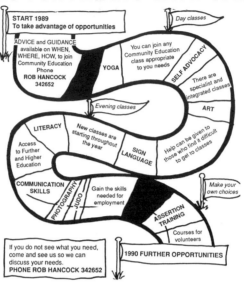

START 1989
To take advantage of opportunities

ADVICE and GUIDANCE available on WHEN, WHERE, HOW, to join Community Education Phone **ROB HANCOCK 342652**

Day classes

You can join any Community Education class appropriate to you needs

YOGA

SELF ADVOCACY

There are specialist and integrated classes

Evening classes

ART

LITERACY

New classes are starting throughout the year

SIGN LANGUAGE

Help can be given to those who find it difficult to get to classes

Access to Further and Higher Education

COMMUNICATION SKILLS

Gain the skills needed for employment

PHOTOGRAPHY

JUDO

Make your own choices

ASSERTION TRAINING

Courses for volunteers

If you do not see what you need, come and see us so we can discuss your needs.
PHONE ROB HANCOCK 342652

1990 FURTHER OPPORTUNITIES

A welcoming invitation from a general prospectus published by South Glamorgan Community Education Service.

Activities at the Grange

The Grange is a small friendly environment which offers a wide choice of creative and basic education classes.

Music
In this class you can learn how to play an instrument and even compose your own song.

Money matters
This class will help you to understand and manage your money.

Extract from Southwark Adult and Community Education's Photo Prospectus

Southwark Adult and Community Education produced a photo prospectus with ILEA and health authority funding to illustrate the available learning opportunities for adults with learning difficulties. Some of the illustrations are shown on page 38.

The *Activities Catalogue* has 112 line drawings of a range of learning activities — from skiing to using a cash withdrawal machine at a bank. The authors suggest that the pictures can be adapted to suit local facilities and amenities. The materials are American and expensive, but worth ordering from a library or sharing. *What's On?* is an British pack which offers a range of illustrated activities for people to choose from, including self advocacy and relationships. (See resources section for further details.)

The Taped Prospectus. Some providers have audiotapes available which outline learning options for adults who have a visual impairment. The same approach can be developed for adults with learning difficulties who have a visual impairment and/or a difficulty with reading.

The Video Prospectus. Video recordings can provide a vivid visual and auditory representation of various learning activities for students to look at and consider.

THE ROLE OF EDUCATIONAL GUIDANCE AND COUNSELLING

It is helpful to spend time thinking and talking before making a choice about what to learn. An initial interview or a review of learning can produce useful opportunities to discuss options, preferences and possibilities.

The role of educational guidance and counselling for people with learning difficulties is an area which is only just developing.

Walsall LEA has recently appointed a project worker for their 'Learning for Living' scheme, which is part of the community education provision. The project worker will develop an educational counselling and guidance service for adults with learning difficulties in the community. In order to access the widest range of opportunities, she will make links and networks across adult, further and community education. Therefore the guidance service will potentially feed into a wide variety of ordinary provision in a variety of educational establishments. Staff development will be an important aspect of the post, as inexperienced providers will require support to take on board the needs of people with learning difficulties.

A small-scale REPLAN initiative is examining how the Bedfordshire Educational Guidance for Adults Network (BEGAN) can adequately address the needs of adults with learning difficulties. This short term project will demonstrate how a service designed for the general public can diversify to cater for the needs of a previously forgotten group.

Organising tutors at Streatham and Tooting Adult Education Institute in London keep aside a day a week for counselling and interviewing students with learning difficulties. The service is optional, but most students choose to make use of it.

> *Think for yourself*
>
> *Do local colleges and adult education centre brochures contain a statement on equal opportunities that positively welcomes students with learning difficulties?*
> *Is the full range of learning options open to students with learning difficulties?*
> *How can information about learning choices be made accessible to students with learning difficulties?*
> *What would the most appropriate formats be for local alternatives to the written prospectus, and what resources are necessary?*
> *Who could help with a photographic or video prospectus — is there an arts centre or college photography department in the area?*
> *What educational guidance and counselling facilities are open to students with learning difficulties, or could be developed?*

HOW CAN STUDENTS MAKE INFORMED DECISIONS ABOUT WHAT TO LEARN?

All adults can make mistakes in choosing what to learn. How many people opt to study a subject of which they have no experience —Russian or sociology perhaps — and find it different from their expectations?

People are best able to make informed learning choices based on concrete experiences. Subjects like French, yoga and photography may be new territory for students with learning difficulties. An experiential approach is the best way for students to decide what they would like to learn.

Taster Sessions

Taster sessions give a sample of various learning activities. Taster days offer a range of subjects for students to sample in the course of one day. Taster courses offer a range of subjects, with each activity being pursued for several weeks at a time.

The advantages of taster sessions are many:

- students can make informed learning choices based on real-life experiences

- students can try a range of learning activities, many of which may be new to them

- tutors offering specialist subjects are often prepared to offer taster courses

- taster sessions can be a useful prelude to integration into an adult education group.

The organisation of taster days and courses is demanding and time-intensive. The risk is that taster sessions may be seen as an end in themselves. There is a need to allocate time for preparation and liaison, while arranging follow-up and progression after the taster sessions is of utmost importance. Once students have made a choice, they will want to pursue their chosen learning options.

Organising Two Taster Days

Preparation: Planning started two months before each day. The liaison and preparation was time-consuming.
Funding: One day was funded by REPLAN. The second day was funded by the local MENCAP society.
Publicity: Pictorial symbols were used to back up publicity for students with minimal literacy skills. The same pictures were used on room doors to help students find their way around and were also used on personalised timetables for each student.
Venue: A large adult education centre was used with a good-sized area for lunch and coffee as well as many work rooms. The venue was accessible by public transport. Transport was offered, but, surprisingly, was not required. The days were held on Saturdays, and many people were dropped off by parents or support workers.
Format: Various subjects were offered by adult education tutors, eight per day. Students could choose a maximum of four activities to try. On offer were yoga, woodwork, French, cookery, art, photography, dance, music, computers and pottery.
Evaluation: Students were interviewed with tape recorders at the end of the day. The feedback was very positive: 'Very good. It was all good. When are we coming again?' 'I learned about sawing properly, which I'd never done before, and how to plane straight.'

Students indicated which subjects they liked best, and wanted to follow up. One non-verbal student was able to show which session he liked best by pointing to the relevant picture on his timetable. Another used Makaton signs to indicate his views.
Follow up: Some students progressed to join integrated classes in subjects ranging from cake making to photography. Other students joined relevant discrete groups of their choice at the local college. A group of students subsequently joined a yoga course at a local community college. Their interest in the subject was sparked off by a taster day.

Think for yourself

How could taster days or courses be organised? Who would need to be involved?
Could taster courses be a regular feature of the provision?
How can students have a say about what subjects are offered in taster sessions?
What options are open to students who have completed taster courses?
How can follow up be planned for, so that choices about learning made on taster days can be pursued?
What are the resource implications?

HOW CAN STUDENTS INFLUENCE THE RANGE OF LEARNING OPTIONS AVAILABLE?

The results of student interviews, taster sessions and reviews may suggest to tutors that new subjects or learning groups should be developed. How can students play a direct role in the planning of provision? Student committees offer one model.

At Streatham and Tooting Adult Education Institute, a student committee comments on provision for adults with learning difficulties. Each group of students with learning difficulties nominates one representative to attend the meetings, which are held twice a term. The students run their own meetings, the agenda of which relates to provision at the Adult Education Institute. Topics include:

• putting in new bids for classes
• reporting back on the classes which students attend
• comments about the Institute's buildings and facilities.

The organising tutors working with adults who have learning difficulties at the Adult Education Institute have made a deliberate decision not to attend the meetings, so that their presence will not inhibit or affect the proceedings. The meetings are recorded by a secretary, who is tutor from a different department.

Think for yourself

How can students have a voice in planning their own provision? What methods can be developed to increase the participation of students with learning difficulties in planning processes related to educational provision?

ORGANISATIONAL ISSUES IN SUPPORTING A STUDENT-CENTRED APPROACH

The models developed will depend on a number of factors in each local area, to include various approaches to:

- policy
- organisational issues in setting up learning options
- multi-agency collaboration.

This section outlines some approaches to organisational issues in determining who learns what —and where. It does not seek to advocate a single package or solution, as to do so would undermine the many and complex issues that need consideration.

Policy

Many individual organisations and authorities have developed or are developing policy statements to guide their work in creating learning opportunities for adults with learning difficulties. In some places excellent work is taking place, but there is nothing on paper to describe their aims. Other areas have policy papers with the thickness and readability of the Yellow Pages, but have developed little in terms of practice. A golden rule in devising policy statements and principles is that they should cover no more than a side of A4 if they are to be adopted and implemented by staff at all levels.

A policy paper on its own is ineffectual unless it has action statements and resources linked to it. There can be many different types of policy:

- individual institution (for example a college or day centre)

- authority-wide, single agency (for example, Local Education Authority or a social services department)

- multi-agency (usually for an authority or region involving two or more of health, social services, education and voluntary organisations; joint care planning statements are district wide) regional (for example the Regional Health Authority)

- national (for example the Education Reform Act).

In *Avon*, a development plan with action statements has been drawn up in relation to non-advanced further education. The paper is being expanded to state who will take what action and by when.

In *Lancashire*, a policy paper on continuing education for adults with a range of special educational needs has been drawn up. Copies were sent to major national organisations for comment and feedback.

In *Sutton*, the local education authority has adopted the policy of 'statementing' for people with special educational needs beyond the statutory limit of school leaving age and up to the age of 30. It is expected that this shift of policy and resources will result in better educational provision for young adults with learning difficulties.

Organisational Issues in Setting up Learning Options

Planning the range of learning options depends on student requirements related to available finance, facilities and staffing. The question of resources is dealt with more fully in Chapter 10. The models of delivery outlined below all allow students to build on existing interests and strengths in developing the learning process. They show different organisational approaches to the process of setting up learning options.

At *Newcastle College of Arts and Technology*, a wide range of choices is available in a menu format. People with moderate learning difficulties can try out anything from calligraphy to bricklaying, often in an integrated setting. General staff are given support and staff development opportunities in order to extend their skills. There is a literacy/numeracy workshop but attendance at this is optional rather than obligatory: students have a choice about whether or not to study these basic skills.

At *Lisson Grove Social Education Centre* in Paddington, 37 options are on offer in the course of a week. The learning programmes are negotiated with students individually. The benefits of this system outweigh the difficulties of a complex timetabling system. Social Services staff are complemented by Adult Education staff in offering various inputs.

At *Northumberland College*, individual action plans are worked out by students in consultation with tutors, based on what they would like to do with their lives. Realistic options are negotiated, and these form the basis of learning programmes. It is a time consuming process, but means that the students are taking control of both their learning and the direction of their lives.

Multi-agency Collaboration

Joint working and joint finance open up new opportunities for the development of educational work with adults who have learning difficulties. Joint care planning is referred to in Chapters 8 and 10.

In terms of increasing learning options, the following initiatives have all been developed. Joint funded posts to develop learning opportunities for adults with learning difficulties. Newham Community College has recently appointed two joint funded education tutors to liaise with day centres and hospitals in order to develop educational provision for adults with learning difficulties. New provision has been set up, including a drama group for black students and a self-preservation course for women.

Co-working between staff across agencies to develop learning activities for individuals and groups. At two long-stay hospitals in Lancashire, computer aided learning centres have been set up. Both are staffed by adult education tutors and nurses working in tandem. As a result,

new technology is being used to develop individual learning programmes for people with profound and multiple learning difficulties.

Think for yourself

Is there a current local policy on education for adults with learning difficulties?
Does the policy state objectives linked to an action plan?
Is it adequately resourced?
Does the policy fit into a broader framework of overall policy on special educational needs and equal opportunities?
If a policy is not under development, could one be initiated?
What models of delivery currently exist for learning?
How could the range and quality of learning be improved?
Is joint finance used to develop learning opportunities?
Do staff from different agencies co-work on learning initiatives?

COHERENT PLANNING

With different agencies offering various learning opportunities, it is easy to find overlap. One young woman joined a cookery group at a social services day centre which she attended. She also did cookery at college. In addition she did cookery at an adult education evening class. There was no contact between the tutors, who were unaware of the threefold duplication.

Multi-agency liaison is essential to use resources to the best effect. Staff from further and adult education are beginning to participate in:

- Liaison meetings. Through such meetings, education services can take an active part in shaping local developments in collaboration with colleagues from other agencies. This can take place at a variety of levels, for both practitioners and managers.

- Individual Programme Plan (IPP) meetings. Education can be integrated into an overall plan rather than operating in isolation. There may be a risk, however, that the educational provision becomes part of the individual's 'day care'.

- Community team meetings for social workers and nurses. In this way referrals can be picked up from community team members working with people who do not attend day services. If this option is chosen, care must be taken to avoid the danger that decisions will be made for/about people by professionals.

- Multi-agency training. Learning together can break down professional barriers. Staff can learn to relate to each other, to share skills and experience — and to speak the same language. Time for liaison should be seen as valid working time for tutors working in further and adult education. One college allows seven hours contact time for liaison to the tutor co-ordinating its care in the community programme.

Think for yourself

What opportunities exist (or could be developed) for creative multi-agency collaboration to widen learning opportunities? How can multi-agency liaison be improved to make a coherent rather than a fragmented delivery of services?
How can time be allocated for staff to liaise across agencies?

SUMMARY AND RECOMMENDATIONS

Colleges and adult education centres should ensure that their publicity contains a statement about equal opportunities and welcomes students with learning difficulties.

All subject areas should be open to students with learning difficulties.

Access to information about learning options should be available for students with learning difficulties in an appropriate format. Consideration should be given to the use of photographic, pictorial and audio-visual formats.

Educational guidance and counselling services should extend their brief to include students with learning difficulties.

Students with learning difficulties should have the opportunity to experience taster days or sessions to make informed learning choices based on concrete experiences.

Student opinion should be taken into account when planning educational provision. Student committees offer one way of eliciting student views.

Policy statements and action plans can be a useful way of creating better learning opportunities for adults with learning difficulties, provided they are actively implemented and adequately resourced.

Multi-agency collaboration can effectively increase learning options by developing creative ways of joint working.

Multi-agency liaison is essential for coherent planning to prevent duplication of learning and wasted resources. Staff involved in education should be allowed adequate working time for liaison across agencies.

FURTHER READING AND RESOURCES

Deborah Cooper *Developing Effective Policy Statements.* Skill (National Bureau for Students with Disabilities), 1987. (Guidance notes for college staff who are developing policy statements regarding students with special educational needs.)

Peter Lavender *Care and Education in the Community. Special Needs Occasional Paper No. 6.* FEU/Longman 1988.

Barbara Wilcox and G. Thomas Bellamy *A Comprehensive Guide to the Activities Catalog.* Brookes Publishing, 1987.

Rod Cragg & Kay Garvey *What's On? A Comprehensive Menu of Ordinary Living Activities for Adults.* (Available only on prepayment of £15.75, payable to R.J. Cragg, from: 302 Station Road, King's Heath, Birmingham B14 7TF.)

4. Ways and
means of
learning

This chapter addresses teaching approaches, techniques and materials. It considers the processes by which practitioners can involve students in planning their own learning.

The steps in learning can be compared to making a journey:

- **Stage 1. Deciding where to go.** Setting aims and objectives for learning.

- **Stage 2. Finding a starting point.** Using assessment as a shared process to guide learning.

- **Stage 3. How will the destination be reached?** Planning learning situations and strategies while taking into account learning styles, modes and materials.

- **Stage 4. Making the journey.** Implementing the teaching plan.

- **Stage 5. Was the journey successful?** Assessing whether or not the objectives have been achieved and evaluating the experience.

- **Stage 6. Where will the next destination be?** Deciding on next steps and routes of progression.

These stages will be considered in detail.

It is important to stress that there is no guaranteed, single or infallible way to teach. Certain strategies/methods/ materials may work for one student but not for another — or may work one week and not the next. Review and re-thinking are critical, combined with a knowledge of general principles about how people learn.

Adults learn more readily when tasks are:

- relevant

- adult rather than childish

- meaningful to their existing experiences

- interesting.

Involvement in all of the stages of learning — from assessment to evaluation — will increase the level of student participation and motivation.

For students with learning difficulties, the process of negotiation and consultation is important, as it is for all adult students. This concept ties in with the theme of self advocacy and empowerment as described in Chapter 2. Ways of involving students with learning difficulties in the learning process are suggested throughout this chapter.

STAGE 1. DECIDING WHERE TO GO. SETTING AIMS AND OBJECTIVES FOR LEARNING

An aim is a long-term goal for students, which is expressed in general terms. For example, students might express such learning needs as:
  'I want to be more independent.'
  'I'd like to get a job.'
  'I need to learn to cook.'

An objective is a specific target to be achieved:
  'I want to sign for my wages.'
  'I'd like to give the right money in the coffee shop.'

These objectives may need breaking down into several teaching steps (see Stage 3).

Setting Aims and Objectives with Students

Ask students what they want to learn and why.

The response may be general ('I want to learn to live on my own') or specific ('I want to learn to write my address').

If several learning goals are mentioned, ask the student to decide which are the most important.

Record this in collaboration with the student if possible. ('I can' and 'I want to' sheets, see pages 50, 51, offer one format.)

If students are unable to communicate their own learning needs effectively, the advice of people who know them well (such as parents, carers and key workers) must be sought. (See Chapter 2 for a description of the role of citizen advocates.)

One example of an individual learning programme record sheet is shown. Detailed records enable progress to be monitored. Information on evaluation approaches can be found in Stage 5.

Individual learning programme record sheet

Name of student:
Skill area:
Aims:
Objectives (numbered and graded in difficulty):
Method/Materials:
Evaluation:
Date:
Comment:

> *Think for yourself*
>
> *How are aims and objectives currently set?*
> *Could the process become more student centred? If so, how?*
> *What record keeping methods would be acceptable and understandable for staff and students?*
> *How can choices be developed for students in:*
> - *deciding what to learn?*
> - *recording their own learning?*

STAGE 2. FINDING A STARTING POINT. USING ASSESSMENT AS A SHARED PROCESS TO GUIDE LEARNING

Assessment is often a process done to, rather than with, a person with a learning difficulty. Much that is assessed is often irrelevant.

Traditional forms of assessment for people with learning difficulties rely on objective tests and extensive checklists which usually highlight a person's weaknesses rather than their strengths. This approach is sometimes described as the 'deficit' model. People are assessed to see what they are unable to do, and are then set 'remedial' teaching programmes designed to fill in the holes. This approach distances the student from the learning process and is disempowering.

Checklists, which tend to concentrate on skills for independence, are very popular with many practitioners. However, they carry the risk that their contents may limit imagination in setting

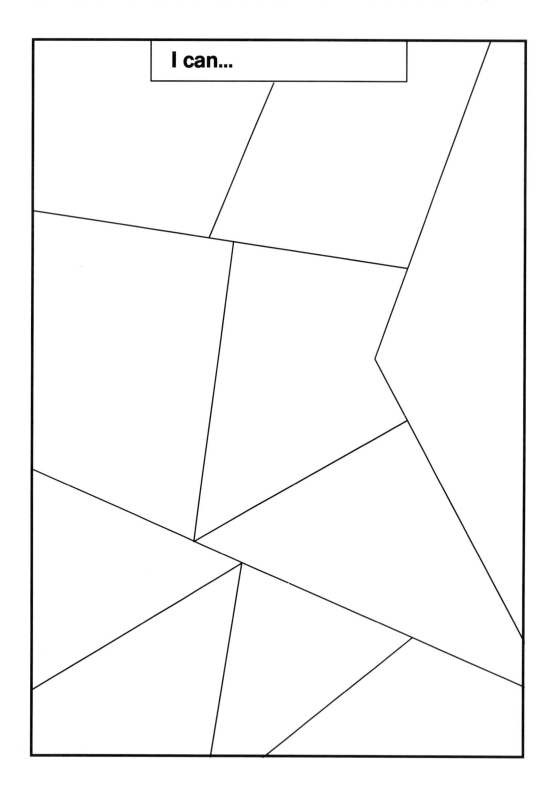

I can...

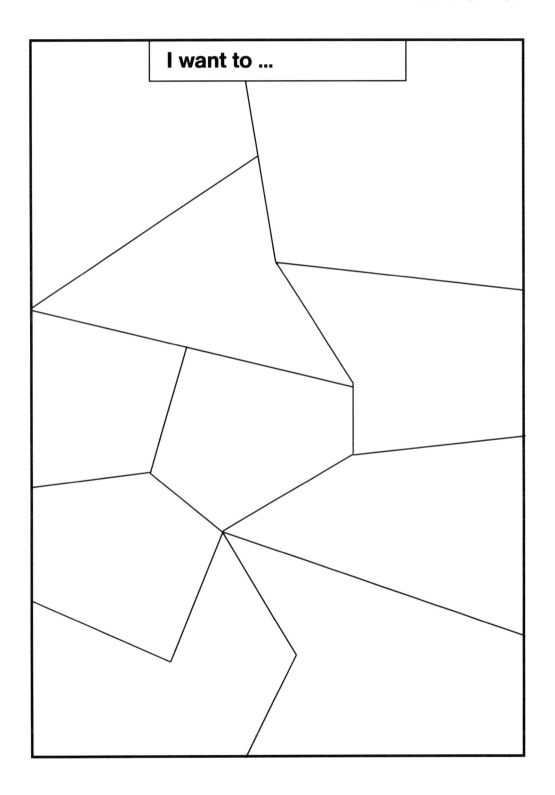

I want to ...

boundaries for learning. One student, when asked what he wanted to learn, said 'I really want to learn about Jesus and history and thunder and lightning!' No checklist on coping skills would have produced that response. Checklists can also limit the planning of learning if they are followed in strict sequence. Staff often teach 'the next step on the checklist' — although it may not be a relevant skill for the student.

Formal assessment by tests and/or checklists may lead to a one sided view of a person. Oliver Sacks (in *The Man Who Mistook His Wife For A Hat*) describes how, in his role as a psychiatrist, he assessed a woman called Rebecca. His tests showed her to be a collection of deficits. It was not until Sacks by chance saw her dancing and also discovered a strong poetic streak in her language that he saw Rebecca as a complete person.

A holistic approach to assessment takes into account a person's interests, strengths and motivation. Making assessment a shared and positive process involves the tutor and student looking jointly at strengths, aspirations and realistic learning goals.

Developing Student-Centred Assessment

Ask students to assess themselves by asking open-ended questions such as:

- What are you good at?

- What do you enjoy doing?

- What would you like to learn or achieve?

- What do you still need help with or find difficult that you would like to develop?

Assessment and recording methods should be student-centred. Page 53 shows a Hampshire ABE profile in which students with learning difficulties are asked to set their own targets. The profile is the property of the students rather than of the professionals. 'I can' and 'I want to' sheets, pages 50 and 51, can record a student's abilities and goals.

Checklists, if used, can be adapted for tutors and students to use together with pictorial back-up. One college adapted a commercial checklist to be student-centred and added illustrations. Students can be encouraged to choose their own starting point. The provision of a wide range of learning materials at various levels will offer scope for students to select their own level at which to work.

Assessment should be used as a basis for learning and development. Some practitioners spend considerable time compiling detailed assessments which are then buried in a filing cabinet and not used to plan teaching. Observation can be helpful in building a picture of a person's competencies and confidence in different situations. Sensitivity and discretion is required so that students do not feel they are 'being watched'. Assessment should be an ongoing process which is part of the evaluation strategy (see Stage 5) and which involves students as much as possible. The language of assessment should be comprehensible to students so that they can assess themselves and understand the learning objectives of the class/course. Assessment results may provide guidance

Target	Date	I should like to be able to:	I know I have reached this target because I managed to:	Date
Practical Skills				
Commnication Skills				
Reading & Writing				
Working with Numbers				
Speaking & Understanding				
Social Skills				
Building up Confidence				

I found it very useful when I was helped in the following ways:

STUDENTS' PERSONAL TARGETS
(From Hampshire ABE Profile)

for future action by both tutor and students or other agencies.

Assessment can:

- identify an individual's strengths and needs

- give guidance on immediate learning priorities

- offer a measure of effectiveness of effort

- provide short-term feedback

- determine the next step.

Assessment can take place at many points during a course, as shown in the model below.

Think for yourself

What methods of assessment are currently used? In what practical ways could assessment become more student-centred?

What happens to assessments? Are they used to plan teaching or stored in a filing cabinet? Who keeps them — staff or students?

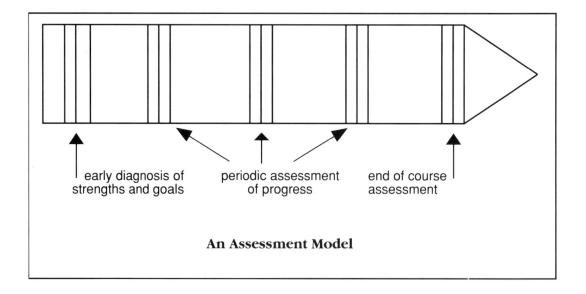

early diagnosis of strengths and goals   periodic assessment of progress   end of course assessment

An Assessment Model

STAGE 3. HOW WILL THE DESTINATION BE REACHED? PLANNING LEARNING SITUATIONS

There are many ways of facilitating learning. This section does not attempt to give a ready-made package, but instead points to a variety of options which can be chosen. The following topics are covered:

- learning situations

- learning strategies

- learning styles

- modes of learning

- materials for learning.

Learning Situations

Student Involvement in Planning Learning Situations. Ask your students for their views and opinions about how and where, as well as what they would like to learn.

A newly-wed couple decided that they would like a short cookery course in their flat. A course was developed which involved collaboration between a community nurse and an adult education tutor. The recipes which the couple wanted to cook were adapted to a pictorial format, and were kept for future reference. The course enabled them to learn skills using their own equipment in a familiar setting.

Students rather than tutors can decide on where to visit, or who they would like as a visiting speaker. One social skills group meeting at Bolton College decided

to go to different hotels in Blackpool for the weekend, and to meet up and discuss how they were getting on with practising their social skills in a real-life situation. The process of students making decisions and planning for themselves develops choice and independence. The process is often more important than the product or outcome. In planning a day-trip to the seaside, students were involved in:

- deciding where to go

- planning the journey and making the necessary phone calls and arrangements

- deciding what activities to do during the day

- planning lunch arrangements

- costing the day.

Tutor Involvement in Planning Learning Situations. The questions the tutor needs to address in planning learning situations are:

Who will be involved? (Tutors, students, volunteers, non-teaching assistants?) Will it be an individual or group activity?

Where will the learning take place? Real-life situations are preferable to artificial ones. Opportunities for integration are preferable to segregation.

How will the learning relate to the past experience of the student? How is the learning relevant to the student's interests and needs?

How does the learning relate to the student's long-term aims? How will the learning be structured, reinforced and transferred?

Why is the learning activity taking place? Is the student aware of the purpose?

When will the activity take place? When will the learning be reinforced?

What learning support materials are required?

Lesson Planning. Tutors training in Avon are given the following outline to guide their planning:

LESSON PLANNING

Ask yourself

1. What am I trying to do?
2. What do I want the students to be able to do?
3. Why do I want them to do it?
4. What standard is necessary?
5. What methods are best?
6. What resources do I need?
7. How do I know that they have learnt something?

Put these all together
Write them down
You have a plan
Now, did it work?

The Readiness Trap Versus Real-Life Learning. Wilcox and Bellamy point out major flaws in the traditional deficit/remedy model. Students are expected to learn isolated prerequisite skills in contrived classroom setting. For example, in learning about shopping people may spend time in the classroom learning to count out precise sums of money, for example £4.59. In reality most of us will give the next pound or note up (£5) and receive change. This is a more useful strategy to learn — and in a real-life situation. Students may also learn to read shopping words and lists. In reality it may be easier for students to take real labels, pictures or photographs to the shop as a cue. Shopping is better learned as a full activity in context, which includes getting to/from the shops, rather than as isolated, component skills in the classroom.

Students are expected to acquire prerequisite skills before being considered 'ready' to go on a trip in the community, for instance, to live in a group home or to enter employment. Why can't the necessary skills be taught in the context of the real-life activity and situation? Transfer of skills will not then present a major problem.

Wilcox and Bellamy describe how the traditional model of cumulative, sequential skill development, which teaches skills in isolation, can be overturned by teaching the whole activity in context and by using appropriate short-cut strategies. A student who cannot perform subtraction can still learn to withdraw a fixed amount of money from a bank cashpoint, while a student without speech can use a communication notebook to learn to order at a restaurant. These strategies will increase choice, competence and independence.

Think for yourself

Where does learning currently take place?
Do students have a choice about where to learn?
Are learning opportunities available

in adult, further and higher education settings?
Do students have an active role in planning their own learning? If not, how could this be developed?
Does the 'readiness trap' prevent students from experiencing real opportunities to develop relevant skills in context?
How can whole activities be taught instead of isolated component skills?

Learning Strategies, Styles and Modes

Research has demonstrated that if teaching is not interesting and relevant to the student, little permanent learning will occur. To retain motivation, the tasks set must be meaningful for the student. This section addresses the various approaches to planning learning. One activity may take in several of these approaches. Everyone has a preferred way of learning, and it can take time to find the best way for a student to learn a new skill.

Strategies for Learning. Students frequently need tasks and information to be broken down into smaller parts in order to assimilate learning.

- Chunking of information into small, digestible parts helps students to understand a subject. Pacing is important as everyone learns at their own pace. To proceed too fast or too slowly is very frustrating.

- Reinforcement and repetition are necessary for learning to be retained. Starting each session with a reminder

of the previous one is useful. Students should be given the opportunity to practise their skills in a range of contexts to ensure transfer of learning. Pitch or level is important to get right. If information is too basic or too advanced, students will become bored.

- Reward and success are encouragements to learning. By making tasks achievable, success can be built in for students with learning difficulties. Reward can be in the form of verbal encouragement (well done! — but not good boy/girl) or any other appropriate form.
Modelling or demonstrating a task is the best way to show a practical skill.

- Language should be clear and unambiguous. As one student commented: 'Some people use too many fancy and technical words.'

- Prompting may be verbal, physical or gestural. This can provide a cue for learning an activity, and can be gradually withdrawn or faded.

- Task analysis provides a framework for reducing tasks to their smallest components. It aims to analyse each separate action so that the sequence can be taught a single step at a time. Decide how task analysis could be used to teach someone to make a sandwich. How many stages are there in this everyday activity?

- Backward chaining uses task analysis in reverse order by teaching someone the latter stages of a task first. For example, in making a sandwich, the last step (putting the top slice of bread on top of the filling) would be taught first. This device is to encourage success in the completed action. Successive stages are then taught until the entire task can be completed unaided.

If the Student is not Learning. If the student fails to learn, the tutor must accept responsibility and needs to critically review the situation, planning and process to see what has gone wrong.

- The learning goal may need to be revised.

- Different teaching methods or materials may need to be employed.

- The pace and pitch of teaching may be inappropriate. Finding the right speed and level to work at is important.

- Background factors (outside noise, tiredness, medication) may be interfering with the student's learning.

- The student may not be motivated or may have reached a plateau in learning.

Think for yourself

Think of one good learning experience you have had in your life — something that you have enjoyed learning successfully.
What factors made it a positive experience?
Think also of a negative learning experience and compare the two. If a student is failing to progress, what

steps can be taken to review the situation?
Is there a key person to whom staff can turn to seek advice, support and ideas to back up their teaching?
Task analysis and Wilcox and Bellamy's view of teaching full activities offer different approaches. Which approach would you use, in which situations and why?

Learning Styles. There are many learning styles, each appropriate for a particular context. Among those widely used are:

- Experiential learning, which is based on real-life experiences.

- Discussion, drawing on the personal experience of the students.

- Reflection, which can follow experiential or discussion-based learning, and allows a chance to think about what has been learnt.

- Demonstration of a practical skill is frequently more effective than a verbal or written explanation.

- Simulation or role play can sometimes be useful to prepare for new experiences.

Think for yourself

Take each of the learning styles described above and consider situations in which their use would be appropriate.
Which learning styles are regularly

*used in local provision?
Are there any approaches which staff
would like to use but feel
unconfident about? If so, who could
help?*

Modes of Learning. There are many different modes of learning. Choosing which ones to use depends on student preference and available resources in terms of staffing, materials, rooms, etc. One group may have several changes of format in one session and may employ several of these modes of learning.

- **Peer teaching.** Skills are shared between students, one teaching another a skill. This enhances the self-image of the student in the tutoring role, and reinforces learning at the same time as they are passing on a skill. A student without speech at the Royal Albert Hospital, Lancaster, taught his friend how to operate a tape recorder by means of gesture and facial expression. The tutor concerned showed skill in standing back to let this learning take place without intervention.

- **Group learning.** A situation in which a group works together towards a common objective. Within this framework, people may be working at their own individual levels. Group work can offer opportunities for communication, interaction, listening skills, negotiation and decision making. Learners in groups often support each other in their learning.

- **One to one learning.** Individual learning between one tutor and one student. SALP in Bedfordshire offer a one to one scheme for learning a range of skills — at home, at an education centre or at a neutral venue. One to one schemes offer great flexibility. Tutors need to be sensitive to issues of dependency, which can be two-way.

- **Drop-in sessions.** Sessions where students can turn up and learn in a flexible way.

- **Open learning.** The use of packs, worksheets, etc. at one's own pace.

- **Distance learning.** Learning at a distance, with occasional meetings with a tutor and phone calls or correspondence in between meetings. Frequency of contact and reinforcement of learning need to be planned for by the tutor.

- **Partnership model.** A tutor works as a partner with a person who has learning difficulties. The Open University course 'Working Together' suggests that a study partner for support is one way of a student with a learning difficulty working through the materials.

At the Northgate Arts Project based at Northgate Hospital, Northumberland, practising artists work alongside residents at a long stay hospital in a co-operative partnership. An artist or a resident may start a piece of work and others are free to join in. There is an interchange of ideas and creativity, with people working as equals on a collective project, taking turns in initiating or developing concepts. Skills are acquired as part of this process — how to work together, how to hold a hammer, how to make choices about materials and colours to use. Wendy Kirkup, an artist working on the project, had observed that someone in her group loved taking things apart. They went together to the dump and retrieved some old record players and fires. The person involved then had a wonderful time reducing these items to their smallest components. This drive was then channelled by his involvement in hanging the pieces from the wooden frame with Wendy to make a remarkable sculpture, which also makes noises when pieces are swung gently together. What was potentially a destructive act had become something wholly creative.

- **Learning together.** Students and tutors can learn alongside each other. Blackburn College organised a course for adult education tutors and former hospital residents to learn Makaton side by side.

Think for yourself

What modes of learning are available locally?
How could the modes of learning be extended to offer students greater choice?
What would the resource implications be?

Materials for Learning

Materials for students with learning difficulties may need to be adapted to take account of the following:

- Some students cannot read and write or have difficulty in doing so. The use of photographic, pictorial and audio-visual materials can support their learning.

- Some students have difficulty with number concepts, which can complicate activities such as telling the time, weighing and measuring. Short-cuts can be developed, such as in cookery using cups for measuring rather than scales or using a talking clock to by-pass difficulty in telling the time.

- Some students have poor memories or trouble with sequencing events. Materials need to be:
  clear and unambiguous
  flexible in use
  real life
  relevant and meaningful
  adult and age appropriate
  durable
  attractive
  well-presented.

A list of selected suppliers can be found at the end of this chapter. Many tutors find that commercial materials are of limited use, and that home-made materials can be tailored to suit individual needs. Many of the best learning aids can be found by using everyday situations to the full, and by responding to individual need and circumstances. Learning to use community facilities needs to be done in context rather than in an artificial situation. Students may like to use their own equipment as aids to learning. Using their own equipment means that transfer of learning is more likely. This could include, for example, resources such as calculators, cameras and tape recorders.

Useful learning support materials can be collected from various sources in the community. A growing number of libraries have a specialist member of staff to respond to the requirements of people with special educational needs. Most local health education centres have a range of materials which can be borrowed. Leaflets from DIY stores, gas and electricity boards, banks and building societies, sports centres, supermarkets, bus and train timetables, menus — all can be a useful resource.

In Walsall's 'Learning for Living' scheme, the post of Resource Worker is being developed for adult education work with adults who have learning difficulties. The job description involves: learning to use equipment in order to support other tutors in its use; developing new learning materials for individuals and for groups; working alongside students and tutors to test and develop new materials.

In Avon, 'Games Galore' is funded by the WEA. People with learning difficulties themselves design, develop and produce games with a learning emphasis. A catalogue is available — see resources section.

Think for yourself

What opportunities are there in your area for accessing the following?
Photographs
Calculators
Books
Cameras
Newspapers and magazines
Videos, video recorders and cameras
Computers, computer software
Slides and slide projectors
Games which are adult-oriented and have a clear learning purpose
Tapes and tape recorders
Overhead projectors
Films/film projectors
Typewriters
Photocopier
Workshop space and equipment
Records/record player
Art, craft and design equipment
Musical instruments
Sports equipment
Gardening tools
Domestic equipment and facilities
Self advocacy materials
Sex education materials
Does your scheme provide a realistic budget for resources?
Is funding available for learning in the community?
Do tutors have allocated time in work hours to prepare materials?
Which specialists could offer skills or learn to share skills?
Is in-service training provided to show tutors:
● *what is in the resource bank?*
● *how to use the materials?*

STAGE 4. MAKING THE JOURNEY. IMPLEMENTING THE TEACHING PLAN

Allow adequate preparation time before students arrive. Keep details of teaching plans in a working file as an overall reminder. It is helpful to have a group plan in addition to individual plans. Planning for individuals operating at different levels within a group context has been compared to spinning plates. It is a challenge that becomes easier with practice, and as the group get to know each other.

Making Learning Successful: Background Considerations

Inside an education room:

- is the room a comfortable temperature?

- is it quiet?

- is the furniture arranged in a welcoming way — circular or in blocks rather than in rows?

- are there attractive, informative displays of an adult, relevant content?

- are learning materials accessible to students rather than locked away; are learning materials clearly laid out so that students can direct their own learning?

Learning to Use Outside Facilities in the Community

Has recent research been carried out about fares, opening times, times of buses/ trains, entrance fees, etc.? Have reminders been sent to students with necessary information about what to bring? Have adequate staffing ratios been arranged for potentially risky situations such as learning to cross roads or learning to use public transport?

Facing Up To Difficulties

Putting into practice what has been planned is sometimes difficult. Flexibility is essential to take account of unexpected circumstances. Tutors often have to change direction or adapt planned sessions at the last moment. The following instances give examples of what can happen.

> *The student fails to arrive. The student may be unwell or have forgotten to come. If the student is not independently mobile, perhaps someone has forgotten to bring him/ her or transport arrangements have broken down. Alternatively, the student may have chosen not to come. The absence will need to be followed up.*
> *The student arrives full of excitement about a weekend trip away. The tutor decides to capitalise on the student's enthusiasm and gives the student the option of doing something related to the recent trip.*
> *The student arrives and has changed his/her mind about priorities for learning. It is possible to draw up a format or informal contract between tutor and student, to say that they agree to work on a pre-arranged topic for so many weeks before*

reviewing options.

The room that the tutor expected to use has been double booked. *Time and energy has to be spent finding somewhere else.*

When the student starts the learning activity, it becomes apparent that the task has been set at too high a level. *A rapid rethink is needed by the tutor, which may mean switching to another activity so that the student does not experience failure.*

The student finds the task very easy. *Further thought is required by the tutor as to what tasks the student can next achieve.*

The group may be dominated by an individual who disrupts learning by behaviour which is distracting. *The group can be encouraged to make a set of their own rules to support learning. Peer group pressure can be more effective than tutor intervention.*

Think for yourself

Are staff allocated time for preparation of teaching?
Are the physical surroundings in the education room conducive to learning? If not, how could improvements be made?
Do students go on trips into the community?
Are these educationally planned and student-centred?
What difficulties do staff regularly encounter when implementing teaching plans?

STAGE 5. WAS THE JOURNEY SUCCESSFUL? ASSESSMENT AND EVALUATION

Assessment offers a way of checking that learning has taken place. When should assessment take place?

- At the start of learning.

- From time to time during learning, to check on progress and retention of learning.

- At the end of the learning process, to ascertain whether objectives have been reached.

Assessment should be a shared and ongoing process between tutor and student.

Evaluation allows for reflection on the experience of learning, and relates to process and feelings. It should take place:

- At the end of each learning session, time should be allocated to a student-centred evaluation activity.

- At the end of a specific period of learning (a short course or a term) it is important to review progress, and to reflect on the value of the experience.

Record Keeping

Keeping good records is of vital importance. Detailed and regularly updated records are essential for planning and review of learning. It is important to consider:

- Who should keep records?

- Who should see records?

- What format should they take?

For learning to be person-centred, the student must take an active role in the process. How can assessment, evaluation and record keeping be carried out in a format which involves the student?
The recording of learning can be done in a number of ways to involve students:

- Written: students with literacy skills can keep a log of progress for themselves. A diary format from Hampshire is shown on page 65.

- Video and photographs: video and photographs can be used to demonstrate the acquisition of skills and experience.

- Audiotapes can be used to record progress.

- Dictation: students may like to dictate information about achievements and feelings for a diary or record sheet. The diary format could be adapted.

- Tick charts: students who can read but not write can tick boxes to describe their progress. An example is given below:
  Can do alone ☐
  Can do with help ☐
  Can't do yet ☐
  Date

- Discussion: the tutor can ask the student's opinion of the learning experience.

- Portfolio: various of these methods

plus reminders of activities can be kept in a file — for example, a seed packet to remind the student of seeds planted, a photo of a chair that has been painted, etc.

- Folders of work can in themselves provide a record of achievement.

- Pictorial evaluations: pictures can help students without literacy skills to communicate their feelings about a session. They can point to or tick the face which is most applicable.

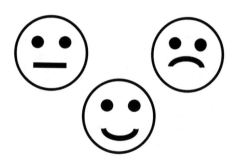

- Review questionnaires: at the end of a period of learning, students can be helped to complete a questionnaire about their perceived progress.

Review questionnaire

Name
Date
I learnt
I feel more confident about
I feel I would like more practice at
I enjoyed doing
I did not enjoy
The tutor could help me by
Next I would like to learn

Date	Today I worked on:	For next time:

Note: 'For next time' can be:
what you need to remember to bring
what you would like to practise some more
what you would like your tutor to bring or prepare

A STUDENT PROFILE
(From Hampshire ABE Profile)

Some of the suggested ways of involving students in assessment and evaluation can be integrated into an overall record of progress or profile. Tutors will find it helpful to have individual records to help with planning. A suggested format is shown on page 49 which combines planning and evaluation.

It is important when evaluating to consider a student's feelings of confidence about skills. A student may be able to perform a mechanical skill, but may lack the necessary self-confidence to complete the task alone. Evaluations should offer students scope to describe their feeling about the learning experience.

Another issue is the appropriate use in context of a skill. Teaching a student to use the telephone involves the consideration of when it is appropriate to use the phone (people tend not to phone each other in the middle of the night unless there is an emergency.)

Teaching and assessment processes should consider transfer of learning. A student may have learnt to use an electric cooker at a cookery class — but if their cooker at home is a different model or a gas one, then the learning will not be easily transferred.

Records of learning should incorporate space for several attempts at a given task, with enough room for a comment to describe how the student got on.

Reinforcement of learning is necessary for a skill to be retained. Problems in memory function or lack of opportunity to practise may mean that a student can complete a task on one occasion but not the next.

What if records indicate a lack of progress?

- The learning objectives may need revision.

- The teaching strategies and materials may need review. Are they suited to the task and relevant to the individual's needs?

- The student may not be motivated to learn, or may have reached a plateau in learning.

- Tiredness, the side-effects of medication, or the impact of epileptic seizures could be factors interfering with the student's learning. Anxiety is another inhibiting factor.

It is the tutor's responsibility to ascertain why a student is failing to learn.

Think for yourself

How do students and staff know when objectives have been reached? Who sets the goals and the standards? Why?

How are reviews carried out for individuals, groups and for the whole service? Who evaluates what, and by which criteria?

Are students involved in record keeping?

What forms of student-centred record keeping could be adopted?

Confidence cannot be measured on a checklist. By what means can staff assess and develop confidence and self-esteem in students?

STAGE 6. WHERE WILL THE NEXT DESTINATION BE? DECIDING ON NEXT STEPS AND ROUTES OF PROGRESSION

The next steps for a student depend on the long-term aims for learning, which may range from being more independent to getting a job or joining a certificated course.

Opportunities should be available for the tutor and student to review possible future options at regular intervals. The tutor needs to be aware of the range of relevant opportunities that exist locally and which can be accessed. One danger is that tutors and students can become locked in situations of dependency, which can inhibit progress, development and forward planning.

Encourage students to think about what they would like to go on to next in terms of follow up and progression to their learning. Some students with learning difficulties have been attending the same adult education class for 10 years. How could they be encouraged to try something new or different? Options include:

- trying a new subject or 'tasters' of subjects

- having a break from learning

- joining a different class or activity

- joining a certificated course.

People with learning difficulties have successfully passed GCSE Art, Cookery (City & Guilds), Horticulture (City &

Guilds), among others. Southwark AEI has prepared an art course validated by the Open College for people with learning difficulties. The Open University course 'Working Together' enables students with learning difficulties to register as Open University students and to complete a course of study. What else can students achieve?

Think for yourself

List all places/courses/activities that could offer possible routes of progression for students.
How can this list be updated?
How can students find out what routes of progression are possible?
How can the 'perpetual student' syndrome be tackled, in which students attend the same class for an indefinite period of time, possibly for years on end?
What certification courses would students with learning difficulties like to join?
What are the barriers?

SUMMARY AND RECOMMENDATIONS

Aims and objectives should be set in collaboration with the student. If the student has serious difficulty in communicating, advice should be sought from parent/carers, key workers and/or a citizen advocate.

Record keeping is essential to chart individual progress and to plan future learning. Student-centred approaches to record keeping will involve and motivate the learner.

Assessment should be a shared process between tutor and student, which builds on strengths and aspirations instead of highlighting deficits. Assessment can demonstrate or check that learning has taken place.

A variety of learning situations, strategies, styles and modes are available.

Flexibility should be employed in determining the most appropriate learning format.

Learning should take place in a real-life situation wherever possible rather than an artificial one (learning to use real money in a shop rather than plastic money in a classroom).

Learning should where possible take place in valued settings used by other community groups and individuals, which offer real possibilities for developing integration.

Evaluation is reflection on learning and relates to feelings and processes. Student-centred approaches to evaluation can be developed, based on a variety of recording methods.

Progression and decisions about next steps require forward planning. Tutors and students should be aware of the range of opportunities available.

FURTHER READING AND RESOURCES

Developing Communication Skills. ALBSU, 1983. (An ideas handbook for tutors working with adults with learning difficulties.)

Lesley Dee *New Directions: A curriculum framework for students with severe learning difficulties.* FEU/NFER, 1988.

Ann Brechin & John Swain *Changing Relationships: Shared action planning.* Harper and Row, 1987.

Jan Alcoe & Hilary Brown *The 5-Star Group: A groupwork pack for developing living skills.* Spastics Society/Pavilion Publishing.

Barbara Wilcox & G. Thomas Bellamy *The Activities Catalog. An Alternative Curriculum for Youth and Adults with Severe Disabilities* and *A Comprehensive Guide to the Activities Catalog.* Brookes Publishing, 1987.

Rod Cragg & Kay Garvey *What's On? A Comprehensive Menu of Ordinary Living Activities for Adults.* (Available only on prepayment of £15.75, payable to R.J. Cragg, from: 302 Station Road, King's Heath, Birmingham B14 7TF.)

Tom Vincent *New Technology, Disability and Special Educational Needs.* FEU, 1989.

Edward Whelan & Barbara Speake *Learning to Cope.* Souvenir Press, 1979.

Margaret Marshall & Dorothy Parker *Read Easy: Reading resources for adults with learning difficulties.* Whitakers, in association with the Book Trust. (This directory of resources includes details of books, audiovisual materials, games and computer software. It is available in book form from Whitakers, 12 Dyot Street, London WC1. Database enquiries: c/o SNRU, Newcastle Polytechnic, Coach Lane Campus, Benton, Newcastle upon Tyne.)

Suppliers of Learning Materials

N.B. Some general educational suppliers have school materials in catalogues. Care must be taken to sift out adult and age appropriate products.

Adult Literacy and Basic Skills Unit (ALBSU), Kingsbourne House, 229—231 High Holborn, London WC1V 7DA. Tel: 071 405 4017.

ALBSU publishes adult literacy and numeracy materials. Some materials are appropriate for use with adults who have learning difficulties, while others can be adapted.

E.J. Arnold. Parkside Lane, Dewsbury Road, Leeds LS11 5TD. Tel: 0532 772112.

Avanti Books, 1 Wellington Road, Stevenage, Herts SG2 9HR. Tel: 0438 350155/741131.

Avanti stocks teaching packs, games, books and computer software. A postal service is available.

Games Galore, c/o Jane Gillard, 53 Sunnyvale Drive, Longwell Green, Bristol.

Games designed and produced by WEA students with learning difficulties.

Living and Learning, Duke Street, Wisbech, Cambs PE13 2AE. Tel: 0945 63441.

Resources for Learning Difficulties, The Consortium, Jack Tizard School, Finlay Street, London SW6 6HB. Tel: 071 736 8877.

Taskmaster Limited, Morris Road, Leicester LE2 6BR. Tel: 0533 704286.

Winslow Press, Telford Road, Bicester, Oxon OX6 0TS. Tel: 0869 244644

Winslow Press have a range of products to include materials for developing life skills and photographs for language work.

Staff Development Packs

Learning Support: A staff development resource pack for those working with learners who have special needs. FEU/ Skill/Training Agency, 1989.

From Coping to Confidence. Staff development materials for staff working with young adults with moderate learning difficulties in further education colleges. FEU, 1984.

The STEP (1985) pack aims to support staff trainers and provides materials on a range of topics including skills assessment, task analysis and writing individual teaching plans. STEP Publications, PO Box 52, Southsea, Hants.

PLAN Publications (1990) have two packs on life planning and needs areas, based on areas common to everyone (such as personal relationships). The approach stresses the active involvement of people with learning difficulties. PLAN Publications, PO Box 1352, Alvechurch, Worcs.

Information Sources

Enquiries about the Hampshire ABE Profile can be made to: Ms Jane Colebourne, Adult Basic Education Co-ordinator, Central Hampshire Community Education Institute, The Pathway Room, Gordon Road, Winchester SO23 7DD.

For information on the use of computers and relevant software with adults who have learning difficulties, please contact: Peter Fowler, National Council for Education Technology, Unit 6, Science Park, Sir William Lyons Road, University of Warwick, Coventry CV4 7EZ.

5. Learning for a purpose

'Learning is fun and interesting. I get active when I come here. I'm more independent too — I've learnt to make the journey.' (Stephen Cole, Student at the City Lit.)

Learning for a purpose is motivating. Whether adults are learning in order to pass a driving test, to grasp a new job or to develop a new skill for fun, the relevance will be enhanced by motivated learning in a real-life situation. Learning which is based on the desire to achieve a personal goal will increase motivation, effort and retention of learning.

This chapter examines various examples of learning in action:

- learning for work

- learning for leisure

- learning for independence

- learning about relationships

- learning for personal development.

The case studies reinforce aspects of practice outlined in Chapter 4.

The distinctive features of the provision described are as follows:

- students are motivated to learn for a particular purpose

- the goals of learning are clear and relevant

- learning is taking place using real-life situations and materials as far as possible

- most of the learning activities outlined involve interaction and integration

with the wider community.

LEARNING FOR WORK

People are motivated to learn new skills for a particular purpose. Learning plays an important role in enabling people with learning difficulties to take up paid jobs in open employment. The advantages are many:

- people with learning difficulties experience gains in confidence and self-esteem when in employment

- earning a wage packet opens up new areas of choice and decision-making — from opening a bank account through to renting a flat

- an integrated work setting gives opportunities for the acquisition of a variety of abilities: from manipulative skills and growth in confidence to the use of public transport

- co-workers learn that people with learning difficulties are 'people first'.

A recent research report by Ann Turner shows the benefit of paid employment from the perspective of people with learning difficulties and their families. The report was carried out for the Welsh Initiative for Specialised Employment, with backing from the Joseph Rowntree Foundation. The survey of jobseekers in a variety of work situations showed that over 80 per cent felt that their lives had changed for the better since they had been working. They said:

'It changed right round because you're getting to know people.'
'I feel better about myself.'
'I've never had money before.'
'It keeps me going.'
'More livelier, more money. It's not really the money, it's the job.'

Parents of jobseekers were also asked, where appropriate, how their sons' and daughters' lives had changed as a result of their experiences in work:

'He sees himself as an ordinary person — working, earning, saving, spending.'
'More grown up.'
'Matured. Takes a great interest in life.'
'Sees himself as more of a man and an independent person.'
'Much more independent.'
'More mature and willing to discuss.'

Three different employment services are described in brief. The first is a social services initiative, the second is a voluntary organisation, and the third is a health authority scheme. They have developed along different lines, and yet have common features. Services of high quality such as those described, which deal with adults with a wide range of learning difficulties, are still few and far between. A participant at a REPLAN Eastern Region conference on employment for people with learning difficulties was enthused by the presentations and asked for the address of the nearest similar scheme. The answer was: 'There isn't one in East Anglia or the East Midlands.'

Blakes Wharf: A Social Services Scheme

At Blakes Wharf Employment Service, run by Hammersmith and Fulham social services department, a team of six employment advisers support people with learning difficulties in finding and keeping the right job. Their experience has shown that it is possible for jobseekers with learning difficulties to exceed staff expectations in terms of the capacity to learn new skills and to concentrate on a task. Blakes Wharf service users include several people who have previously been excluded on the grounds of 'challenging behaviour' from special schools and day centres, and some people who communicate in Makaton. Individual attention when a new job is being learnt, coupled with ongoing support and flexible staff hours, mean that over 40 people have successfully found and kept jobs. These range from catering and working for British Airways to painting and decorating. Some of the people first placed in work are now progressing to supervise other members of staff in their job settings. In addition to the 40-plus people already placed in jobs, an additional 40 people are looking for work with Blakes Wharf support.

The staff input is undoubtedly very intensive, especially when a person is starting to learn both a new job and how to use public transport. A Blakes Wharf employment adviser can put in up to 70 hours a week on these occasions. Time off in lieu can be taken, and a good staff network offers much-needed encouragement and support. A method called systematic instruction is used for teaching people new skills in work settings, which encourages success at every stage and 'fading' of staff input as confidence develops. The staff are emphatic that work experience rarely leads to a 'proper' job, and will negotiate wages for all work undertaken.

For further information, contact: Blakes Wharf Employment Services, 147 Stevenage Road, Fulham, London SW6.

The Welsh Initiative for Specialised Employment (WISE)

WISE is a voluntary organisation, which was started in 1985 on the initiative of a group of parents and a social work student. WISE is currently funded through the All Wales Strategy. It provides opportunities in:

- work experience
- sheltered placements
- open employment
- Employment Training — both for people with learning difficulties and for people who want to work with them
- setting up co-operatives shared by people with and without learning difficulties.

For further information, contact: The Director, Welsh Initiative for Specialised Employment, 10 St Helens Road, Swansea SA1 4AN.

Intowork in Sheffield

In Sheffield, the Intowork scheme caters for residents in health authority hospitals and hostels, many of whom are institutionalised and have challenging behaviours. The scheme is run by occupational therapy staff, and was set up by psychologist Mark Feinmann in 1987. An employment development officer co-ordinates the scheme and liaises with employers to find paid work opportunities for people with learning difficulties. Four job trainers support approximately 20 people in their work-settings, helping them to learn the necessary skills and then gradually withdrawing from the situation.

Finding the right job to motivate a person with a challenging behaviour has in many cases stopped incidents of headbanging, swearing, spitting, shouting and self-mutilation, which can be caused by frustration and boredom. Jobs have been found in a number of settings — factories, hospitals and a bakery.

By concentrating mainly on individuals with challenging behaviours, the scheme is both giving an opportunity to a group frequently denied the chance to work, and is also demonstrating to employers and co-workers that people with very severe learning difficulties are capable of making achievements in the field of work.

People from long-stay hospitals often have stereotyped views of the jobs they want to do: gardening for men and cleaning for women. Actual experience is the best way to find out about a job and several jobs may be tried before the right one is found — as is the case for most people, whether disabled or not. For further information, contact: Employment Development Officer, Intowork Employment Services, 119 Manchester Road, Sheffield S10 5DN.

FEATURES COMMON TO EMPLOYMENT SERVICES

- Flexible staffing enables job trainers to work variable hours according to the nature of the job they are teaching, and the speed at which a person learns the necessary skills.

- Job trainers work at a job on their own for several days before introducing the person with a learning difficulty to the situation. This enables them to fully understand the requirements of a job, in terms of both work and social skills.

- Use of task analysis and 'systematic instruction' breaks a job down into easily-taught steps.

- Individual negotiations with the Department of Social Security are currently necessary for each person, to investigate levels of benefits and wages that can be earned. This can be time-consuming and frustrating. Where people are resident in private homes, finding wages to match residential fees and outgoings is a difficulty.

Applejacks: A Training Environment

Applejacks is a small, friendly café serving home-made food in an ordinary street in Camden Town. It provides training for people with learning difficulties to learn how to prepare and serve food to customers in a real-life setting. The menu pad is specially designed to be used by people who may have minimal literacy skills. Applejacks has produced a manual to explain how the training café was set up. Contact Applejacks at: 255 Eversholt Street, Camden, London NW1.

Education Towards Employment Project

In the North-East, an interesting initiative is developing supported work training for people with learning difficulties. It aims to bridge the gap between existing further education provision for adults with learning difficulties and the goal of employment. The project is the result of collaboration between Newcastle University, North Tyneside College of Further Education and North Tyneside Social Services Community Mental Handicap Team. Funding has been obtained from the Employment Service Inner City Programme Development Fund. For further details contact: Anne Baynes, North Tyneside College of Further Education, Embleton Avenue, Wallsend NE28 9NJ. Tel: 091 262 4081.

Think for yourself

Jot down all the different professionals across agencies who are involved locally in developing work opportunities for adults with learning difficulties.

How can adult and further education support employment initiatives? How can new employment initiatives be set up?

Who would need to be involved? What would the resource implications be?

> *Is there someone with experience of the education and training needs of adults with disabilities on the local Training and Enterprise Council (TEC) or on its sub-committees? If not, could a TEC member be invited to attend the local committee for the employment of people with disabilities? (Ask your Disablement Advisory Service manager for committee details via the Jobcentre.)*

LEARNING FOR LEISURE

Research by MENCAP has shown that many people with learning difficulties have solitary and passive leisure pursuits, such as watching television or doing puzzles. Learning can play an important role in developing skills and relationships in relation to the use of spare time. Three different examples of learning for leisure are described in the following sections.

Leisure Integration Project

London MENCAP runs a Leisure Integration Project. A survey in 1988 showed the narrow range of leisure options experienced by people with learning difficulties. The then project co-ordinator, Rachel Sutcliffe, devised a four-point strategy for improving opportunities:

- Building up a photo library of leisure activities. (This stage was not realised due to a shortage of funds.)

- Organising taster visits to clubs and societies.

- Organising short courses. For example, a bowling club offered tuition for people with learning difficulties.

- Arranging for integration into community events, such as the Richmond Festival of Sport.

'Leisure Links' schemes are being set up which link a person with a learning difficulty with a volunteer to integrate them into ordinary clubs. The recommendations of the project have been adopted by Sutton Recreation Services, who have appointed a full-time leisure integration co-ordinator for people with learning difficulties. Further information about the Leisure Integration Project is available from: The Development Officer, Leisure Integration Project, London MENCAP, 115 Golden Lane, London EC1Y 0TJ.

> *Think for yourself*
>
> *What leisure opportunities are currently open to adults with learning difficulties locally? What new opportunities could be developed? What role would learning play? Who would be involved?*

New Opportunities and Experiences in a Rural Area: The Community Living Skills Group

Karen Davies is the Adult Basic Education organiser for North Shropshire. The 'Second Chance' programme caters for a approximately 400 adults, of whom an estimated 100 have moderate or severe learning difficulties.

A major challenge was to find ways of meeting appropriately the needs of adults with learning difficulties who live in remote rural areas. The Community Living Skills group was established in 1987 and meets once a week during term time. The group meets for two hours on a weekday evening.

Target Group. Members of the group were identified in collaboration with the local social services department and the health authority who now jointly fund the work. The target group invited to join were seven people who led very sheltered and isolated lives in the rural areas. Some of them had stayed full-time in the family home, and never been out, spending their time helping their families with household chores. All were in their late twenties or early thirties.

Aims of Group. The aims are to give opportunities to develop friendship with others, and to encourage the use of local leisure facilities. The group members themselves decide on the programme, which develops choice, decision making and confidence.

Transport. Karen Davies carefully researched the issue of transport. Under the 1985 Transport Act, every local authority has a duty to provide transport accessible to the disabled. The local authority, when prompted, offered to pay for taxi fares for people with disabilities to get to and from adult education groups.

Karen's next aim is to adapt a taxi to cater for people who find difficulty in climbing in and out of vehicles. Social services and the Cadbury Trust also contribute to the substantial costs of providing individual transport in a rural area. A short article by Karen Davies, 'Getting a move on: transport, access and legislation', appeared in *Adults Learning*, March 1990.

Staffing. Two tutors experienced in Adult Basic Education co-tutor 'The Community Living Skills Group'.

Programme. The students themselves decide on the activities, planning half a term in advance. The activities have a social bias and have included:

- trips to a local pub, where the group have joined in with playing pool

- planning and preparing a barbecue, to which friends were invited

- going swimming at a leisure centre

- going out for a meal at a restaurant.

New Experiences and Opportunities. These everyday activities were brand-new experiences to many of the group, who have led very sheltered lives. The following steps towards independence were taken:

- one person had to buy his first pair of swimming trunks at the age of 35, as he had never tried swimming before

- another person so enjoyed the swimming that he plucked up the courage to go by himself the following week: 'I felt a bit nervous, but I knew it would be all right because I'd been before'

- some of the group had never before eaten a meal away from home until the group went out to eat at a restaurant.

New Confidence in Social Skills. People who were shy and withdrawn have developed self-confidence. They are now pleased to introduce themselves and to chat in a relaxed way to new people in a social situation.

Think for yourself

How does local provision address the issue of transport for people with learning difficulties?
Does local provision include rural areas? If so, in what ways could the social and educational needs of adults with learning difficulties living in the rural areas be addressed?
How can social education be planned and evaluated with/by students?

Shared Learning Experiences in Outdoor Activities

Jim Casey is a social worker who devotes his free time to developing outdoor pursuits for adults with learning difficulties and their parents and carers. His philosophy is that having to survive in the natural environment helps people to learn to understand themselves psychologically as well as developing new

physical skills and building trust and confidence. When staff and parents see an individual with a learning difficulty acquiring skills and overcoming perceived risks, it can enhance their perceptions of what a person can achieve.

Jim's approach has been to take parents/carers and staff away for several weekends, so that they can gain experience and confidence in a range of activities:

- abseiling

- canoeing

- rock climbing

- caving

- walking

- camping

- orienteering.

Role boundaries change and relationships develop as staff and parents jointly experience rope assault courses and night rescue exercises. They develop to the point of knowing what they can achieve with comfort and safety.

The next stage involves a weekend with staff and parents working alongside people with learning difficulties. Participants are not excluded by any selection criteria, and several people with profound and multiple learning difficulties have taken part in the activities outlined above — for example, experiencing abseiling in a wheelchair. Participants can choose from a range of activities, which are pursued at their own pace.

The benefits are many:

- parents/carers and staff extend their own personal development and learning

- the knowledge and confidence they gain is used to enable people with learning difficulties to acquire new skills and experiences

- images, roles and expectations all change and develop as people support each other through new experiences

- people work as a team towards shared goals and learn to trust each other in physically challenging situations.

Jim Casey has to fund-raise via grant applications because outdoor activities, with their specialist equipment, are expensive. Staff training costs for mountain leadership courses and residentials have also been met by fund-raising. The whole project rests on Jim Casey's enthusiasm, drive, initiative and spare time. Despite approaches to statutory agencies, he has had no luck to date in securing ongoing funding, while his active involvement is not seen as compatible with his day-to-day work as a social worker in a Community Mental Handicap Team.

Think for yourself

Could your agency support an initiative like this?
How flexible are local agencies in terms of financing and supporting innovative learning schemes?
Are joint learning experiences provided for staff, parents/carers and

adults with learning difficulties?
What possibilities exist for developing outdoor pursuits as a part of learning programmes for adults with learning difficulties?
How accessible are sport, leisure and outdoor pursuits for people with profound and multiple learning difficulties, both in the local area and further afield?
What health and safety issues need to be considered in relation to outdoor pursuits?

LEARNING FOR INDEPENDENCE

'I've had no training at all! I've learnt how to look after myself by watching other people do it. I've made a few mistakes — like burning holes in my shirts and burning saucepans.' (Michael Cook, adult education student.)

Nobody is competent at all everyday living skills — least of all when they first leave home. People develop ways of getting round personal difficulties, whether it's ringing the plumber to tackle a dripping tap or expecting someone else to regularly cook meals. How many people leave home without feeling worried about everyday tasks such as cooking or budgeting? People with learning difficulties are often expected to 'jump through hoops' and to be ultra-perfect at everyday chores before being given the chance to be more independent.

One hospital 'rehab' unit taught its residents to make a habit of hoovering under the sofa every day. Residents also had to wash up breakfast dishes every day before going to work, or else they were financially penalised. How many people in the community live up to these artificially high standards? People with learning difficulties are subjected to hours of 'domestic training'. The equipment they are using is often different from the equipment that is available in their own homes or anticipated new accommodation. This disparity creates problems in the transfer of skills learnt. People are often 'selected' for training rather than choosing it as an option for themselves.

One day centre manager decided that ticking boxes on skills checklists was not the best way to decide who was 'ready' to live in the group home. Instead, a notice went up and a message was broadcast — who would like the chance to live in a group home? People who responded were interested, motivated and enthusiastic.

Think for yourself

How did you acquire personal skills for independence?
What do you still find difficult?
How do you get round this?
What level/standards are students with learning difficulties expected to reach? Is this realistic? Do they have any choice? What ongoing support will be available?
Does home skills tuition take place

using domestic equipment that the student is familiar with, and will have the opportunity to use in future home life?
How is learning reinforced?

LEARNING ABOUT RELATIONSHIPS

'Simple acts of hospitality — buying a round of drinks, making a cup of tea — are all the stuff of acquaintanceship. With time, people unused to these skills are able to learn them.' (Ties and Connections.)

Friendship

Self advocates talking about friendship:

'Friends talk to you.'
'They are very important to have when you live alone.'
'Friends can help each other out.'
'If you are in a bad mood and you feel terrible, you can talk to friends.'
'Friends are nice. If you make them you can go out with them.'
'You have got to mix with people and to know who your friends are.'
'It is good to have friends and relatives.'

Opportunities for new friendships for people with learning difficulties can be restricted. Some people have spent years together at school and then spend years together at a segregated day centre. In all probability, they go to the same segregated leisure club as well. How can learning situations maximise new opportunities for social development?

- At Skills for People, self advocates design and run courses about making friends.

- One adult education group in Avon met for two terms. In the first term students looked at 'Making Friends', while the second term took the theme of 'Keeping Friends'. The ending of friendship was also discussed.

Integrated settings open up new possibilities for friendships. People learning in work settings or in integrated adult education schemes have been invited to parties, weddings and meals out with colleagues or other students:

'I'm learning to get on with people and to mix in. I've got lots of new friends now.' (Self advocate working at a supermarket.)

Knowledge and experience of leisure options open up social possibilities. At the Paddington Integration Project, a 'What's On' board displays information and publicity about local events. Students are encouraged to learn to go out to social events, with flexible staff support if needed.

Reciprocity

One student with a learning difficulty clearly recognises that friendships are reciprocal when he says:

'It's a two-way thing. I help old age pensioners with shopping in bad weather. They help me by giving me advice.'

A community resource worker running a befriending scheme in Salisbury felt strongly that shared interests were the best way to develop friendships. In one instance, a man living in a group home enjoyed woodwork and had his own tools, but there was no one to help him to develop his hobby. He was introduced to a retired widower who was good at woodwork, and who was delighted to share his skills. Both of them enjoyed the activity and the company. The other people in the group home like baking cakes and having visitors for tea — so all of the group home residents and the widower benefited from the mutual arrangement.

Making Arrangements

Social skills are necessary to develop and maintain friendships. Real-life situations are the best way to foster these skills. An adult literacy group in Bristol for people with learning difficulties regularly met at the local library. The group decided to have a Christmas party. The students were actively involved in:

- choosing the venue

- deciding who to invite

- deciding what to eat and drink

- preparing the food.

A discussion took place about how to make visitors welcome. Suggestions included:

- shaking hands or hugging guests

- taking people's coats

- offering drinks and food

- talking to shy people

- asking people to dance.

The conversation highlighted the social skills which would be necessary — and had extra significance because it related to a real-life situation which the students had been involved in planning for themselves.

Arranging to meet friends may require the development of certain skills, for example:

- using the telephone

- planning and making a journey

- arranging a time and place to meet

- decision-making in relation to what to do: for example, choosing to meet for coffee, to go shopping or to go to the cinema.

Other ways of keeping in touch with friends may also offer scope for learning:

- to write notes and letters or to make tape-recorded messages

- to send greeting cards for special occasions

- to write postcards.

One adult education student with a learning difficulty writes an annual letter to his brother in the Midlands, to ask if he can go and stay for Christmas. This is the only letter he writes every year, and is very important for keeping in touch with his family.

Think for yourself

What opportunities can be developed for people with learning difficulties to learn about friendship?
How can suitable courses be developed with students to meet their stated needs?
Is there a group of self advocates who could design and mount a course, as 'Skills for People' did?
What is the potential role of learning in befriending schemes?
How can real-life events/occasions/ festivals involve students in order to capitalise on learning social skills in a relevant way?

Relationships and Sexuality

Community nurse to newly-wed man with learning difficulties: *'If you want to talk about sex education, I can help you.'* Newly-wed: *'Oh — it's alright, Jane, the dog sleeps in between us.'*

Policy and practice on sex education for adults with learning difficulties vary widely across the country. Concern about political sensitivity and parental anxiety means that in many places, sex education is taboo:

'We tried it once — a few years ago. The local paper picked it up and ran an article headlined "Sex for people in the twilight world". There was so much opposition that we had to stop.'

In some areas, sex education has been put 'on ice' while policy documents are drawn up at County Hall level. Responding to individual need and finding appropriate resources can be a major problem. A social worker and an adult education tutor tried everywhere without success:

'In the library, the adult books about sex had the pictures cut out. In the children's library the books were locked up! Anyway, they were unsuitable. The Health Education Council had a video of people romping nude on the beach, which wasn't a good role model. In the end we decided to try and produce our own materials about sexuality and AIDS. We had the ideas, but we couldn't get funding.'

Ann Craft of the University of Nottingham is currently researching and piloting appropriate methods and resources for sex education in collaboration with parents and staff from various agencies, working with adults who have learning difficulties.

Why bother teaching about sexuality?

People have a right to information about relationships and sexuality. People who are ill-informed about sexuality and their personal rights may be at risk in a variety of ways, for example sexual abuse, an unwanted pregnancy, or the danger of contracting VD or AIDS.

The WEA (Western District) provides free 10-week sexuality courses for men and women in two stages. Stage I operates as single sex groups. Stage II can be studied in single sex or mixed groups. Transport has been provided for those who need it. Students are welcome to bring a friend/supporter of the same sex with them if they choose to do so. Newham Community College is running a course on health issues for lesbians with disabilities. It is hoped to recruit women with a range of disabilities, including learning difficulties.

Think for yourself

What are the difficulties and challenges which face staff, and relatives/carers in facilitating sex education for adults with learning difficulties?

What opportunities/resources are available locally for people with learning difficulties to learn about sexuality?

If the situation is unsatisfactory, how can it be improved? Who would need to be involved? What are the resource implications?

How can relatives/carers be supported in coming to terms with a sex education programme for their adult sons/daughters?

What staff development is needed for staff to feel at ease with teaching sex education?

> *How can staff work across agencies and share skills in order to effectively deliver a coherent programme of sex education?*

LEARNING FOR PERSONAL DEVELOPMENT

Learning can be fun! People with learning difficulties have successfully participated in a wide range of learning activities for self-development and interest:

- tap dancing
- yoga
- art
- photography
- cake making
- massage
- French
- electronics
- car maintenance.

Gerald expressed the desire to learn to ride a motorbike. Parents and day centre staff threw up their hands in horror and forbade him to learn because of the risks of a traffic accident. A community resource worker spent time talking to Gerald, who explained that he wanted to ride a bike over the farm fields with his brother, near where he lived. He did not actually want to take the bike on the busy roads nearby. The resource worker acted as a go between. As a result, Gerald enrolled for tuition at a motor-cycle school. He now rides his own motorbike.

> *Think for yourself*
>
> *What have you always wanted to have a go at learning but never got around to? Why?*
> *Ask students the same questions. One student trying art for the first time, said 'I didn't know I was allowed before'.*

Carousel: A Creative Arts Project

The Carousel Project is based in Brighton, and runs a range of creative arts activities for people with learning difficulties, which involve the wider community wherever possible. Activities are advertised as being for people with and without learning difficulties. Music, voice, movement, art and drama form the basis of Carousel's work. Wherever possible, sessions are held in everyday venues rather than segregated centres for people with disabilities. A musician who can improvise on various instruments adds a rich dimension to movement sessions. The motions of the participants can be instantly translated into a suitable musical accompaniment.

The work of the four key staff is funded by grants from year to year, often for specific projects. A Care in the Community grant enabled a group of parents/carers of people with learning difficulties to make a video about their experiences. For more information contact: Sarah Jackson, Carousel Project, 2 St George's Place, Brighton BN1 4GB.

> *Think for yourself*
>
> *What opportunities for creative education are available?*
> *How could they be expanded and funded?*

SUMMARY AND RECOMMENDATIONS

Services should ensure that they make adequate provision in the following areas and should use student's interests, strengths and motivation as a key factor in planning for:

Learning for work in a community setting.

Learning about leisure opportunities in the local community.

Learning about relationships and friendships (to include information on sex education as appropriate).

Learning for independence in real-life situations.

Learning for personal development, to include creative arts, learning a subject for fun or to fulfil an individual personal goal.

FURTHER READING AND RESOURCES

Resources Related to Employment

The Employment of People with a Mental Handicap. Progress towards an ordinary working life. King's Fund Centre, Project Paper Number 55, 1985.

Employment Opportunities for People with Severe Learning Difficulties. An information pack. King's Fund Centre, 1989.

Enabled to Work. Support into employment for young people with disabilities. FEU, 1989.

Building on Ability. A guide for training people with disabilities. Training Agency, 1989.

Special Needs, Special Opportunities. Conference report available from NIACE REPLAN Office, YHAFHE, Bowling Green Terrace, Leeds LS11 9SX.

A report of the REPLAN Eastern Region 1989 conference on employment for adults with learning difficulties is available from: REPLAN Field Officer, Eastern Region, Phoenix Chambers, Castle House, 15—17 High Street, Bedford.

Information about Training in Systematic Instruction (TSI) and relevant courses is available from: Mark Feinman, Secretary, TSI, Department of Clinical Psychology, Olive Mount Hospital, Old Mill Lane, Liverpool L15.

Information about Training Agency initiatives for people with learning difficulties is available from: Training Agency, Policy & Programmes Division, Moorfoot, Sheffield S1 4PQ. Tel: 0742 593404. Addresses of local Training Agency Area Offices can be found in local telephone directories. The local Disablement Resettlement Officer and Disablement Advisory Service can be contacted via the nearest Jobcentre. They can provide the following: *Code of Good Practice on the Employment of Disabled People; Employing People with Disabilities:* various booklets; *It Can Be*

Done, a video on managing employees with a range of disabilities.

Details of the MENCAP Pathway Scheme are available from: 169 City Road, Cardiff CF2 3JB. Tel: 0222 494933.

Deb Steele of Excel Employment, 2 Hornsey High Street, London N8 (tel: 081 348 8141) offers a newsletter, staff development workshops and consultancy.

Resources for Leisure/Outdoor Pursuits

Mike Cotton *Outdoor Adventure with Handicapped People*. Human Horizons Series, 1983.

For work in rural areas, consult: *Country Matters: A development worker's guide to supporting unwaged rural learners*. NIACE REPLAN, 1989.

Jim Casey took people to Bendrigg Lodge. Contact: The Bendrigg Trust, Bendrigg Lodge, Old Hutton, Kendall, Cumbria LA8 0NR.

RADAR provides a factsheet on outdoor activities and holidays for people with disabilities. Contact: RADAR, 25 Mortimer Street, London W1N 8AB. Tel: 01 637 5400.

Resources for Independence

Pictorial shopping lists are available from: The Consortium, First Floor, Jack Tizard School, Finlay Street, London SW6 6HB.

Cooking By Picture Recipe Cards. Available from: Dr Sue Shackleton Bailey,

Hampshire Social Services, Trafalgar House, The Castle, Winchester SO23 8UK. (Cost £6.50 +postage.)

Step-by-Step Cookery Book. This pictorial recipe folder, prepared by dietitians in Southmead health authority, is available as follows: Edition I available from Sergeant Brothers Printers Ltd, Unit 9, Pontyfelin Road Industrial Estate, New Inn, Pontypool, Gwent NP4 0DQ. (Cost £5.00 including postage and packing.) Edition II is available from Gloria Simmonds, Administration Department, Brentry Hospital, Charlton Road, Bristol BS10 6JH. (Cost £6.00 including postage and packing.)

Resources for Friendship

Ties and Connections. King's Fund Centre, 1988.

Jodie Walsh *Let's Make Friends*. Souvenir Press, 1986.

Ann Richardson & Jane Ritchie *Developing Friendships*. Policy Studies Institute, 1989.

Socialising is a discussion pack for adults with learning difficulties which looks at four aspects of socialising, including going to a pub and going to a party. Published by: Living and Learning, Duke Street, Wisbech, Cambridgeshire PE13 2AE.

Resources for Sexuality

Michael & Ann Craft *Sex and the Mentally Handicapped. A guide for parents and carers.* Routledge and Kegan Paul, 1985.

Hilary Dixon *Sexuality and Mental Handicap. An educator's resource book.* Learning Development Aids, 1988.

Ann & Michael Craft (eds) *Sex Education and Counselling for Mentally Handicapped People.* Costello Press, 1983.

Ann Craft (ed.) *Mental Handicap and Sexuality: Issues and perspectives.* Costello Press, 1987.

Michael Gunn & Joyce Rosser *Sex and the Law: A brief guide for staff working in the mental handicap field (England and Wales only).* Family Planning Association Education Unit, 1987.

Not a Child Anymore. (Teaching pack for adults with learning difficulties.) Brook Advisory Centres, 1987.

Between Ourselves is a video of women with learning difficulties speaking up about sexuality. It is aimed at women. It is available for hire or purchase from: Twentieth Century Vixen, 82A Lordship Lane, London N16 0QP. Tel: 01 802 3911.

Educating Mentally Handicapped People. Set of teaching slides developed by Ann Craft. Cameral Talks Limited, 197 Botley Road, Oxford, OX2 0HE.

Ann Craft *Health, Social and Sex Education for Children, Adolescents and Adults with a Mental Handicap: A review of audio-visual resources.* Free resource list available from the Health Education Authority.

Winifred Kempton slides. American slides about sex education. Distributed by Concord Films, 201 Felixstowe Road, Ipswich, Suffolk IP3 9BJ. Tel: 0473 7266012.

Women and Health. Activities and materials for use in women's health courses and discussion groups. WEA North Western District/Health Education Council, 1989. Available from: WEA Publications, 9 Upper Berkely Street, London W1H 8BY.

The FPA run courses for staff and produce their own material on sexuality. Contact the FPA, 27—35 Mortimer Street, London W1N 7RJ.

Ann Craft of Nottingham University is currently researching and piloting appropriate methods and resources for use in sex education programmes for students with severe learning difficulties. She is working with staff from schools, FE colleges and adult settings. Newsletters are available from her at: Department of Mental Health, Floor E, South Block, Queen's Medical Centre, Nottingham NG7 2UH.

Resources for Arts Projects

The Arts Council produces an annual
*Directory of Arts and Disability
Organisations and Projects.* Available
from: Arts Council, 105 Piccadilly,
London W1V 0AU.

6. Integration

Segregate: *To set apart: to seclude: to isolate: to group apart.*
Integration: *Unification into a whole, e.g. of diverse elements in a community, as white and coloured.*
Participation: *To have a share or take part in.* (Chambers Twentieth Century Dictionary)

Integration has been a buzz word in services for people with learning difficulties for some time. The sharing of ordinary places and activities with other people is an unarguable value. To exclude a person with a learning difficulty from everyday life on the basis of their disability is isolating and inhuman. It perpetuates the myth that 'these people need to be kept separate.'

This chapter focuses particularly on integration in an adult or further education context. Integration opportunities in wider situations are described in Chapter 5, 'Learning for a Purpose'.

There are three distinct aspects of integration:

Locational integration — the sharing of places and buildings. In educational terms, this means gaining access to colleges and adult education centres. A central location within the building confers value on students with learning difficulties. In reality, how much 'special needs' provision is tucked away in a shabby Portakabin at the back of the car park?

Social integration — social mixing, for example at mealtimes and breaks. In colleges and adult education centres, lunch and coffee breaks are often central to the 'hidden curriculum' in which learning to queue and pay at a cafeteria or to use a vending machine plays an important role for students with learning difficulties who are developing social skills. In some cases, social interaction with other students can be extremely limited. Students in general do tend to stick to their own groups: how often do the engineers and the hairdressers or the French and the biology students mix?

Functional integration — joining in with activities alongside other people. It is the move towards integration in learning situations that has been most challenging for providers. *Education Observed*, a report by HMIs, comments that 'there is scope for planning more opportunities for integrating students with special needs into mainstream courses.'

The following sections describe two educational developments in integration for adults with learning difficulties.

THE PADDINGTON INTEGRATION PROJECT

This project is an example of full-time education for adults aged 21—24 which offers a range of options for integration.

The Paddington Integration Project (PIP) was set up in 1983 when parents became concerned that their son would be leaving Paddington College at the age of 21 without the opportunity to continue his education full-time. The idea of developing a course to consolidate and extend learning opportunities for young adults with severe learning difficulties became a reality with a grant from the Conoco oil company, which launched the project.

Currently the project is financed by a mixture of fund raising, donations and local authority grants. It is sited at Beauchamp Lodge, a community centre which houses a number of other projects with which PIP has close links, in particular the adult literacy scheme, nursery and café.

The Students

The students are aged between 21 and 24 years. Many of them have attended full-time provision until the age of 21 at Paddington College, although referrals are accepted from a variety of sources. Most of the students have severe learning difficulties. They can attend PIP for two years full-time and can return part-time in the third year. Between 12 and 14 student places are available at any one time.

As the project is currently sited in a flat on the top floor of a building without lifts, mobility is a factor in the criteria for course entry. Parents and students must also be willing for travel training to take place, with the eventual aim of independent travel.

The Staff

Four members of staff run PIP. They come from a variety of backgrounds including adult literacy and the health service. All are committed to developing a student-centred curriculum. The good staffing ratio coupled with the freedom to work flexible hours means that a variety of individual and small group work can take place in a range of settings at different times of the day and sometimes during the evening.

The Programme

Publicity about the programme is available in two formats. One is aimed at prospective students, while the other is provided for parents and professionals.

A project management group of parents and professionals oversees the running of PIP. The group has mostly been concerned with the financial situation, but plans are underway for the management group to have more involvement in the overall direction of the project.

The Curriculum

The curriculum is student-centred and provides a variety of opportunities for integration. There is a clear emphasis on choice, decision-making and the development of confidence in an atmosphere which is adult and relaxed. Each student has an individual programme, both within the building and outside in the community. Options range from a choice of study topics at PIP to a choice of adult education, work experience and leisure activities in the community. At a weekly student meeting, which is chaired by the students themselves, students discuss recent and future activities. Staff also have the chance to pass on new information at this meeting.

Activities at the PIP Flat

Opportunities are available by choice to develop self advocacy, literacy, numeracy, drama and social skills. Students can opt to join groups on health and sex education, which have the full backing of parents. A mixture of visual aids and group discussion is used to develop students' understanding and awareness of various facts and issues, including AIDS. Individual counselling is available to talk through a student's needs and interests.

The PIP flat is sited at the top of Beauchamp Lodge Community Centre. The students eat and mix with other centre users in the ground floor cafeteria, and some students do work experience in the kitchen. A recent donation gave scope to redecorate the flat. The students were actively involved in the process, which gave an opportunity for developing practical and cognitive skills.

Links with Adult Education Centres

PIP has close links with three Adult Education Institutes in the area. The activities on offer are discussed with PIP students, who then decide what they want to learn and where. The groups on offer are usually a mixture of discrete and integrated provision, offering special provision or a chance to join open groups. PIP staff then help the students to learn to make the necessary journey, and offer individual support as required. PIP students have chosen to take part in a wide range of adult education classes, from gardening to car maintenance.

Integration in Work Settings

One aim of PIP is to provide a range of work experience options for students so that they can make an informed choice about the sort of work they would like to do. The staff are responsible for finding out what sorts of jobs the students would like to try. They then try and find appropriate placements, and offer support

to employers and students during this time. Recent placements include:

- working in the warehouse of Marks and Spencer

- fronting the reception desk at St Mary's Hospital, Paddington

- office work in a council building

- working with animals in a children's playground

- canteen and café work

- Beauchamp Lodge nursery.

The students are pleased to describe their work placements and proud to show visitors photos on the wall at PIP of themselves at work. Many students develop part-time jobs through this scheme, which they continue after leaving PIP One is currently working two days a week as a hotel porter. Staff at PIP have close links with employment agencies and Jobcentres, and some students have progressed to full-time employment.

Integration in Leisure Settings

A student 'What's On' board has a display of various activities, concerts, exhibitions currently on in London. From this a student might form a plan for going out with a friend for an evening. PIP staff can follow this up, offering graduated support in learning how to plan, make arrangements and travel across London.

The flexible hours that PIP staff work mean that a member of staff can be available for these evening activities, which offer a valuable alternative to the segregated leisure clubs which many people with learning difficulties attend. An annual holiday for PIP students gives a focus on planning a trip away, which involves many skills.

Progression from PIP

After two years full-time at PIP students can choose to return for a third year on a part-time basis, in order to continue their education while exploring other options. Most students, when they leave PIP, move on to a part-time paid job coupled with part-time attendance at adult education groups of their choice. Four have found full-time open employment. It is estimated that only two students who have been on the PIP course have taken up places at social services day centres.

Think for yourself

How could a project such as PIP be funded in terms of accommodation, salaries, materials and travel expenses?
How could its effectiveness be evaluated?
How could staff be enabled to work flexible hours to cover evening and weekend learning activities?
How can integration projects with segregated bases ensure that there is an emphasis on progression and moving on and out into integrated settings?

INTEGRATION INTO ADULT EDUCATION PROVISION

'It was really good. It was really great, it was. I enjoyed it. Learning to use all the different computer programmes. I used Dial-A-Ride to get there. There's people you haven't met before — meeting new people is good.' (Mark Biddle, student at a community college.)
'It's quieter learning at the community college than at the day centre. It's too noisy at the centre.' (Stephen Thompson, student.)

Following the pioneering work in Islington and Hillingdon, financed by MENCAP in 1981, a number of schemes have developed to enable people with learning difficulties to participate in adult education provision on an integrated basis. The central issues have emerged from the belief that people with learning difficulties have citizens' rights to attend adult education provision alongside other students. To exclude a student on the grounds of race or gender is unacceptable. To exclude a student because of their learning disability is equally unacceptable.

In order to make participation for students with learning difficulties a reality, additional and flexible support is necessary.

Student Support

Support for students choosing learning options should be provided. See Chapter 3, 'Learning Choices', for descriptions of taster sessions and visual prospectuses. Additional support in the integrated situation will maximise learning. Support can be provided by a co-student, volunteer or additional tutor.

Staff Support

Tutors new to working with adults who have learning difficulties will need support, guidance and advice. Individual support and training opportunities are required. The following comments by adult education organisers reinforce this need:

> *'Some tutors say yes, they'll gladly take a student with a learning difficulty. Then they spend the whole summer worrying.'*
> *'One tutor agreed to take a young woman with learning difficulties in her flower-arranging course. The tutor was fine at first — but then turned against the student, and eventually excluded her. I did what I could, but I felt awful.'*

One scheme has developed a positive approach to attitude change and staff development. Staff working on an integration project at Thamesside and South Greenwich Adult Education Institutes in London developed a flexible staff development programme for full-time and part-time tutors new to working with adults with learning difficulties. Tutors chose between a two-hour session, which covered the basics, or a nine-week course of two hours a week, which went into more detail. The longer course involved inputs from staff working for other agencies, to put the work into a multi-disciplinary context. The take-up rate for training has been good.

Volunteer Co-student Support

It is a point of debate whether or not volunteers need training in order to accompany someone to an adult education class. One scheme organiser decided that: 'It isn't necessary to know the history of adult Training Centres to go to a pottery class with someone.'

Initial support is certainly essential, and most scheme organisers spend time with new volunteers, explaining the scheme and the approach which is needed. Written advice is helpful, and one example is shown. Ongoing support is usually offered both through personal contact and by telephone. In some cases, where attending a training course is optional, integration volunteers have elected to take part.

INTEGRATION PROJECT INFORMATION

Aims of the integration project
1. To provide access to adult education groups for people with learning difficulties. This will be done by pairing a student with a volunteer co-student, matching interests if possible. The tutor will be approached by SALP initially. Tutors and volunteer co-students will be offered advice and support on an informal level as well as at termly meetings.
2. The scheme will enable students who have learning difficulties to share ordinary places and ordinary activities with other people. This is a learning experience in itself, and can promote social confidence, as well as

giving students a chance to develop new skills.

3. The scheme will also give other group members a chance to relate to and interact with a person who has learning difficulties. The best model the volunteer and tutor can provide is to treat the student as an adult and as an equal.

Role of the Volunteer

1. To give practical help e.g.
- *working out coffee money*
- *finding way around building*
- *possibly travelling together.*

2. To give personal support
- *by working alongside the student*
- *by giving encouragement.*

The level of support/help needed will depend on the student's abilities.

3. To act as a bridge if needed
- *between the tutor and the student*
- *between the student and the rest of the group.*

Classes will be free to volunteers and students. Volunteers can claim travelling expenses.

Transport

Transport is a major barrier to access for students to travel independently. Volunteers, minibuses, Dial-a-Ride services and taxis have all been used to enable students with learning difficulties to reach their adult education groups. Clapham and Battersea Adult Education Institute appointed a transport liaison worker to work five hours a week on counselling students with disabilities and arranging suitable transport. Funds were obtained to provide two buses and a full-time driver/helper for adult education students, and a local charity provided a second driver.

Accommodation

Adaptations to buildings may be needed to enable students with learning difficulties and physical disabilities to gain safe access to classes and facilities. One student with learning difficulties is regularly carried up and down a long and steep flight of stairs in his wheelchair by the organising adult education tutor, so that he can reach his adult literacy class. This situation has gone on for six years. It has taken numerous requests to get official permission to put in a new door at ground level to offer proper wheelchair access. The request has finally been approved, but the work has yet to be done.

Health and Safety

The above example highlights health and safety aspects which must be considered in facilitating safe and dignified access to classes. Staff may need training — for example, in how to lift someone from a wheelchair, or in how to handle a wheelchair.

Fees

Policy on fees varies from one local education authority to another. In many cases, because the majority of students with learning difficulties are unemployed, there will be full or partial remission of fees. Volunteer co-students are usually given 'free' places on the basis that they are attending in an enabling role.

Naturally, points of view vary:

'Students with learning difficulties should pay at least something if other people do, so that they are participating on equal terms.' *'If we advertise that classes are free for co-students, it could attract the wrong sort of person. Bring a disabled person and come free — it sounds all wrong.'*

The payment of fees should not present a barrier to learning for adults with disabilities, who are often in difficult financial circumstances.

The Readiness Trap

Many schemes have developed elaborate routes for students with learning difficulties to pass through before being considered 'ready' to join an integrated class. The arguments for segregated 'bridging' courses in Adult Education Institutes as a pre-integration phase are that:

- they give a chance for students to develop skills and try out new subjects

- they provide an opportunity for students to get to know their way around the adult education building, and to mix at coffee time.

The major difficulty is that people often stay in these groups, and do not move on and progress to integrated provision. They get 'stuck' in the system.

The Literacy Debate

Adult literacy students in general often have low self-esteem and poor self-image. Charnley and Jones (*The Concept of Success in Adult Literacy*) suggest that a growth in self-confidence is necessary before skills can develop. Adult literacy organisers are acutely aware of the anxiety and embarrassment that students attending adult basic education can experience. They are perhaps admitting to others for the first time that they find difficulty in reading, writing and spelling. It is for these reasons that the integration *en masse* of students with severe learning difficulties into adult literacy provision is a sensitive and difficult topic. It is one to which there is no easy solution.

One scheme has offered a range of literacy opportunities for adults with learning difficulties. Some students with moderate learning difficulties have successfully integrated into an evening class with support. Other students receive one to one tuition from full-time or voluntary tutors. Some special literacy classes run in colleges, where students have joined the libraries and made use of the facilities. Another literacy class offers integration in reverse. It was originally set up for students with moderate or severe learning difficulties. Three 'mainstream' literacy students elected to join the class because they preferred its slower pace. All of these options were chosen by students themselves — which demonstrates the need to offer literacy provision which is wide-ranging, flexible and student-centred.

Much of the good practice observed during the project was being implemented by tutors with a background in adult basic education. They had successfully transferred approaches from adult literacy, including negotiating with students and starting at the individual student's preferred level. These tutors were also experienced in the selection and use of adult materials.

INTEGRATION IN ACTION

This section describes a range of initiatives which aim to develop integration in an adult education context. The pioneering work financed by MENCAP in Islington and Hillingdon in 1981 generated interest and enthusiasm for the integration of people with learning difficulties into adult education classes. Schemes vary in format and delivery from one area to another. Common to all is the need for extensive liaison and groundwork, which is highly labour intensive.

The preceding section provides the theoretical background. Putting integration theory into practice is both complex and challenging, as the following case studies illustrate.

Integration in Action: Croydon's Experience

In September 1988, Croydon Local Education Authority created the post of Integration Development Officer. The post was designed to expand integration into adult education provision, and followed on from a successful part-time initiative at Ashburton Centre, where the six hours a week allocated had proved inadequate in response to a growing demand for integrated provision. Bonnie

Tandy is the full-time post holder at the time of writing.

Approximately 90 students with special educational needs are currently integrated into adult education classes in Croydon. About 60 students have learning difficulties, which tend to be mild or moderate. About 30 students have their involvement facilitated by a volunteer co-student. The others attend without additional support. Volunteers are hard to come by. Publicity is displayed at the three main adult education centres on enrolment day in order to attract potential volunteers. Bonnie has developed an annual cycle of events to structure her work:

April/May: Students with learning difficulties are interviewed to ascertain their learning goals. Students are referred from a variety of sources, including day centres, group homes, the local MENCAP society and parents/carers. Travel possibilities are explored. Some students can already travel independently and some will learn the new route to an adult education centre. Others are transported by volunteer co-students.

June/July: Once the needs are identified, work starts on matching students up with appropriate classes, and with a volunteer co-student if needed. Tutors are contacted at home and students' names are put on class lists. There is a large postal enrolment, and if Bonnie does not reserve places, the classes are likely to be full.

August: A general guide to courses is published and widely distributed. It contains a welcoming statement for people with disabilities — and also asks for volunteers.

September onwards: Classes start. Bonnie circulates, making informal visits to each class to check that all is well with tutor, student and volunteer (if there is one). She is available for phone consultations and personal meetings if necessary. Students who are not sure about a new subject are welcome to observe a class to see if it is what they expect or not, before committing themselves to joining in.

Croydon is a reasonably compact area, and most of the integration work is focused on three adult education centres. Other sites are used, but some present difficulties in that they are isolated and offer no coffee facilities. People with learning difficulties enjoy the same wide variety of learning options as other members of the community, with whom they share joint experiences as adult learners. People with learning difficulties are currently participating in integrated classes in Croydon which include:

- trampolining
- family history
- ballroom dancing
- car maintenance
- jujitsu self-defence
- practical first aid
- photography
- cookery
- table tennis
- art and pottery.

Most of Bonnie's time is taken up with liaison and co-ordination of the integration work. She also works with the special needs co-ordinator to organise in-service training sessions for tutors and volunteers involved in special needs courses and integrated provision. Sessions on special educational needs are also a feature of general tutor training courses. In addition, Bonnie draws on her experience to contribute to general working parties on various aspects of adult education. A policy on provision for adults with special educational needs is currently under development.

Think for yourself

How could a full-time integration post be financed and supported in your area?

Integration in Action: A Rural Area

In contrast to Croydon's urban programme co-ordinated by a full-timer, Heather Andrew has just two hours a week to negotiate integration in Leighton Buzzard, a small town whose adult education facilities are used by people in the surrounding rural areas.

Transport has been a major headache. Two volunteers from rural areas were willing to help, but transport problems proved insurmountable. Despite an intensive publicity campaign, few volunteers have come forward.

So far, Heather has arranged the successful integration of five students with learning difficulties into a range of classes over a two-year period, often working beyond her two paid hours a week. It has been a slow and time-consuming process. As Heather says: 'It sounds so easy and straightforward but it all takes so long.'

Think for yourself

How can issues of transport be addressed in your area?
Is it realistic to expect of a member of staff to work on integration on such a part-time basis as this?
If volunteers use their own cars, are expenses paid?
Is insurance cover provided for volunteers?

Integration in Action: Adults with Profound and Multiple Learning Difficulties

An integration project at two adult education institutes in London (Thamesside and South Greenwich) has focused on adults with profound and multiple learning difficulties returning to the community from Darenth Park Hospital.

The students have no verbal skills, and require constant attention. For this reason, each student is accompanied by a support worker from his or her group home. The first year has been spent introducing students and support workers to new activities and taster sessions in discrete groups at the adult education institutes.

Project worker Cilla Stanbury explains that under an equal opportunities policy, the students have a right to receive continuing education regardless of the severity of their disabilities. Their presence within the adult education institutes has given the work a high profile with other centre users and staff. Timing of classes and transport have both been obstacles. Saturday morning sessions have proved popular. Group homes are often well staffed at weekends, and a Saturday session also saves protracted negotiations with health or social services day centres. Flexibility about exactly who attends from which group home has also been helpful, as the students tend to have a high sickness rate. Physical access has limited the choice of rooms which students can use. Activities have included cookery, craftwork, aromatherapy and music/movement.

Staff training has been well attended (see page 94 for a description). In Cilla's opinion, despite a supportive environment, it will 'take ages' before students with profound and multiple learning difficulties can share classes with non-disabled learners.

Southwark Adult Education Institute asks support workers from group homes to accompany on a one to one basis students with severe or profound learning difficulties who are institutionalised following many years in hospital before returning to the community. Southwark staff have devised a training course for support workers to enable them to support students with learning difficulties effectively in a learning situation.

Think for yourself

What opportunities are offered for people with profound and multiple learning difficulties to integrate in adult education activities?
How can physical presence and social mixing be extended to enable shared participation with other adult learners?

Integration in Action: From Discrete to Integrated Provision

Chris Wilcock, co-ordinator of the Grange Art Centre at Southwark adult education institute, has devised a five-point plan of progression by which students with learning difficulties develop from discrete to integrated provision. Classes are offered in the following environments:

1. At the social services day centres in discrete, closed groups. This provides a familiar, known environment in which people can experience learning.

2. At the Grange Art Centre in discrete groups but with social mixing with other centre users before and after classes.

3. At classes open to all adult learners at the Grange, where students mix with people from the community both in class and out of class.

4. At other adult education sites in the area, in discrete classes but with students travelling independently.

5. At other adult education sites in the area, at mainstream classes with students travelling independently to mix with other adult learners.

Chris Wilcock prefers to use the phrases 'participation' or 'full participation' in preference to the word 'integration'. The word 'participation' to her means joining in on equal terms, whereas 'integration' implies that the students with and without learning difficulties are radically different, which they are not. Volunteers are not used in the Southwark scheme, as the organiser feels that this would make the students with learning difficulties stand out more. Instead a learning support tutor is on duty at the institute to provide back-up if needed. Chris feels that students themselves must feel ready and willing to join a mainstream group. Currently 40 students have taken up this option.

Think for yourself

How can phased schemes like this one encourage progression to ensure that students don't get 'stuck' in the readiness model?

Common Elements in Adult Education Integration Schemes

- A keyworker is designated to have responsibility for overseeing the integration scheme. This person may work for health, education or social services, or may be joint-financed. The role may be full- or part-time.

- Volunteers are usually recruited to accompany a student with learning difficulty to an adult education class. Media publicity, posters, leaflets and requests to students enrolling for classes have all been used as recruitment methods.

- Matching of the volunteer co-student with an adult who has a learning difficulty then takes place according to a variety of factors: shared interest — this gives a point of contact; geographical considerations — student and co-student may choose to travel together to the class; availability during the day or evening. An initial meeting gives the chance for student and co-student to meet and get to know one another. If after this meeting, the pair both wish to proceed, then student and volunteer co-student join the adult education class and work alongside each other. It is the role of the co-student to give the right level of support to the student with a learning difficulty to enable them to participate in the learning situation. This may range from practical support (finding their way round the building) to encouragement and support to develop confidence.

- Volunteer co-students are given advice and written notes about relating to their student in a positive, enabling way. An example is shown.

ADVICE FOR VOLUNTEERS

1. Be aware that the way you talk to your student will often set the tone that others in the Adult Education Group might follow. Treat him or her as an adult and therefore try to avoid talking down to your student when showing him or her how to do something.

2. Everyone needs encouragement, therefore concentrate on the things your student can do well. The more one fails, the less motivated one is to succeed. Therefore, help your student complete a task successfully BUT not by doing it for them.

3. On introducing your student to others, there is usually no need to explain that he or she has learning difficulties.

4. Be careful not to talk about your student in his or her presence.

5. Try to find ways of helping other people accept your student. By showing others your acceptance of your student for what he or she is, others might be encouraged to do so.

6. Be careful not to impose your own values and likes upon your student. This may be difficult, because whilst it is important to ascertain what his or her likes or dislikes are, many people who have learning difficulties may not have had the opportunities to express themselves. Therefore give them opportunities to do so.

7. Try to find subjects in common with your student as a basis for exchange of ideas.

8. Help your student to understand the complex area of social skills, i.e. learning to listen to others and take turns in conversation, allowing for other people's feelings, how to initiate approaches to other people.

You can contact us at any time to discuss any aspect of your involvement as a volunteer.

(Amended from original guidelines by Jacquie Billis.)

- References on volunteers are usually taken up. This process safeguards the student with a learning difficulty and the professional reputation of the scheme.

- Participating mainstream tutors are offered guidance and support.

Elements Particular to Certain Integration Schemes

Some schemes have adopted individual ways of working which other areas may like to consider.

- A social lunch to share ideas. The organiser of the New Ways scheme in Hampshire organises a termly ploughman's lunch for volunteers and tutors. This occasion offers a chance to share successes and worries in an informal supportive atmosphere.

- Video to demonstrate scheme. An integration scheme in Central Norfolk

called Link Up has made a video of its work as a record, which is used to explain how the scheme works.

- Integration facilitated by a member of the Community Mental Handicap Team. The health service-funded resource worker at Salisbury Community Mental Handicap Team facilitates integration at Salisbury College. There is a long-term aim for students with learning difficulties to progress to the point of being able to participate in the class without the accompaniment of a volunteer wherever possible. Five out of nineteen students have so far achieved this goal. The resource worker is available on a paging system in case of difficulties or emergencies at the college. An information sheet informing all parties concerned of the arrangements is distributed to ensure good communication.

VOLUNTEER CO-STUDENT SCHEME

Information Sheet
Student name and Address: Rosalind, Salisbury, Wilts
Volunteer name: Ann, Salisbury, Wilts
Class: Pottery for All
Course: A407074, 20 weeks commencing 30.9.88
Venue: Tollgate T.16
Time: 9.30—11.30am Friday
Special Needs: Roz has very little hearing and communicates by a few simple signs and gestures. In the case of an emergency Roz would require

physical prompting. She also gets upset if she is unsure what is happening but responds to someone gently explaining by mime and pictures.
Transport: Ann will collect Roz from home and return her either to the Adult Training Centre or home according to weekly requirements.
Co-ordinator: Janet Marsh, Community Resources Worker, Tel: Sals 336262 (Ext 3109/3110); In emergency Sals 332347. (In either case you may get an answerphone, but I will ring you back as soon as possible.)

Salisbury College of Technology: Salisbury 23711
Copies to: Rosalind; Ann; Janet Marsh; S Centre; Noelle; Tutor

- Integration at a sixth-form college. The Peter Symonds College in Winchester is open to adult learners of all ages, as well as to sixth formers. A full-time integration worker is developing educational opportunities for adults with learning difficulties based on interaction with teaching staff and other students. To date, adults who have moved back to the community from hospitals and special school leavers have benefited from the arrangement. Students have integrated into a wide range of subjects — from basketball and screen printing to electronics and current affairs. They have helped with the college newspaper and shop, and joined in with activities to include canoeing, swimming, climbing, cycling and skiing.

- A full-time integration post in Wales. Funding from the All Wales Strategy for people with learning difficulties has been used to fund a full-time education integration worker in Mid-Glamorgan. The post holder is developing integration in adult education centres and youth clubs, as well as making positive links with comprehensive schools which offer community education for adult students.

SUMMARY AND RECOMMENDATIONS

For a successful integration experience, the following will be necessary considerations:

- staff development and support

- additional support for the student in the learning situation if required (the role of the support person will vary according to individual need)

- support for volunteer co-students

- attention to physical access to buildings for students with learning difficulties who have physical disabilities.

The payment of fees should not be a barrier to education for students with learning difficulties.
   Provision of transport (or learning to use transport) as necessary. Time to negotiate placements — whether in education, work, leisure centre, etc.

Flexible staffing hours.

A review process is necessary both for individuals and for the scheme overall.

FURTHER READING AND RESOURCES

Chris Lloyd *A Realistic Goal? Special Needs Occasional Paper No 5*. FEU/ Longman, 1987.

Jacquie Billis *A New Way — From Theory to Practice*. MENCAP, 1984.

Penny Willis & Chris Kiernan *A New Way Evaluated*. MENCAP/Thomas Coram Research Unit, 1984.

Julie Care *A New Way — Five Years On*. MENCAP, 1986.

Education Observed. Students with Special Needs in Further Education. Department of Education and Science, 1989.

Integrated Adult Education for People with Learning Difficulties. MENCAP London, 1986. (A resource pack comprising slideshow, cassette tape and booklet: only booklets now available.)

Regular Lives, a video showing integration in a range of settings in America, is available from Values Into Action.

Jane Colebourne *Report on the Continuing Learning Centre, 1989/90*.

Copies of this report (£2 inc. p&p) available from: Jane Colebourne, Adult Basic Education/Special Needs Co-ordinator, Central Hampshire Community Education Institute, The Pathway Room, Gordon Road, Winchester SO23 7DD.

7. Students with learning difficulties and additional complications

Some students with learning difficulties have additional complications. This chapter highlights particular circumstances in which learning must be tailored to take account of the factors that complicate it.

In many areas, adults with learning difficulties and additional complications are denied access to learning. The education service does not adequately cater for their needs. The examples given in this chapter seek to demonstrate that access to learning for people with learning difficulties and additional complications is a right that can be realised. The main topics covered are:

- Teaching language and communication skills.

- Teaching adults with profound and multiple learning difficulties.

- Teaching adults with severe learning difficulties who have visual and auditory impairment.

- Teaching adults with challenging behaviours.

- Teaching students in a secure environment.

TEACHING LANGUAGE AND COMMUNICATION SKILLS

A number of adults with learning difficulties have some kind of complication related to skill acquisition in the area of language and communication:

- difficulty in making basic needs known, especially for students with profound and complex learning difficulties

- lack of spoken language

- poor articulation, resulting in unclear speech

- delayed language development, resulting in telegrammatic speech ('I go shops' instead of 'I am going to the shops')

- difficulty with concepts of language (for example, prepositions such as: on, under, in)

- limited receptive language, as understood by the student when communicated *with*. Students may say 'yes' and smile as if understanding, when in fact they do not understand but wish to please

- limited spoken vocabulary (or expressive language) as communicated by the student

- difficulty in sequencing of events

- problems in short- and long-term memory processes. The last words said to a student may be the only ones remembered in some cases.

Communication skills may be developed by:

- the appropriate use of a structured language programme based on individual needs and transferred to everyday situations

- the use of an alternative language system based on signs or symbols as a means of communication

- the use of communication aids which staff at Communication Aid Centres will match to suit the needs of each individual

- the encouragement of self-expression by developing opportunities for communication and discussion.

Seeking Professional Help

Speech therapists are employed by district health authorities. They receive a four-year professional training in the development of language and communication skills. Most areas employ specialist speech therapists to work with adults who have learning difficulties. Referrals can be made via the health authority. In cases where a speech therapist is unable to work directly with a person, advice on methods and materials can usually be obtained to suit individual needs.

Structured Language Programmes

Language programmes usually come in a pack which includes communication assessments with defined teaching goals and methods outlined. Three examples are briefly outlined below. Their advantage is that language programmes offer a highly structured approach to the teaching of communication skills. However, the majority of schemes are written for children and require adaptation of materials and vocabulary to suit the needs of adults. Generalisation of skills learnt will not happen spontaneously. Careful planning is needed to ensure that formal sessions carry over into everyday situations in order to reinforce learning.

The Communication Assessment Profile (CASP) (1988, Anna Van der Gaag).

CASP is clearly aimed at adults with severe learning difficulties. The three assessment booklets are for individual completion by a carer and a therapist, while the third is a joint assessment. A ring binder presents material with age appropriate black and white photographs. Published by Speech Profiles Ltd in association with Speech Therapy in Practice. Details from: Speech Profiles Ltd, 25b Thames House, 140 Battersea Park Road, London SW11 4NB.

The Derbyshire Language Scheme. The Derbyshire Language Scheme has been used widely with children who have severe learning difficulties and is also popular with staff working with adults. The use of dolls furniture and a childish vocabulary present difficulties in its use with adults. People using the scheme with adults tend to adjust it to age appropriate activities and vocabulary. Staff are asked to attend a three day training course, or to use the pack with guidance from an approved tutor. An adaptation for adult students is currently in preparation. Details from: Area Education Office, Grosvenor Road, Ripley, Derbyshire. Tel: 0773 7447411.

Early Language Training Programme. This language programme is child-based, though it could, with imagination, be adapted for adults. The main advantage is that it starts at a very early developmental stage, making it particularly suitable for people with profound or severe learning difficulties. The format consists of a card index box with coloured cards, each listing a separate communication skill with a teaching plan. Details from: Drake

Educational Associates, St Fagan's Road, Fairwater, Cardiff.

Sign and Symbol Communication Systems

Various sign and symbol systems are used with adults who have learning difficulties who either have no speech or who have unclear or limited speech. It is important to consider individual needs when deciding which system to adopt.

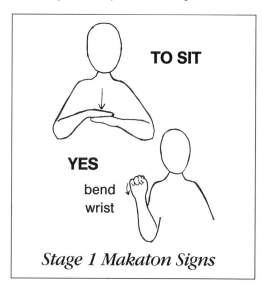

TO SIT

YES
bend
wrist

Stage 1 Makaton Signs

Makaton. Makaton is an adapted form of British Sign Language which was developed by speech therapists. It is widely used with and by people who have learning difficulties. Training in the precise signs is important so that regional variations do not develop. Local Makaton representatives can advise on training courses, and can be contacted via the address below. Makaton relies on hand signals and requires a certain level of manual dexterity. Information from: The Makaton Vocabulary Development

Project, 31 Firwood Drive, Camberley, Surrey.

Blissymbols. Bliss is a system which uses symbols that can be pointed to on communication boards. Blissymbolics is a visual, meaning-based communication system. Some of the symbols are pictographs, which look like the things they represent.

General enquiries and orders for materials can be made to: Mrs Ena Davies, National Co-ordinator, The Blissymbolics Communication Resource Centre (UK), Thomas House, South Glamorgan Institute of Higher Education, Cyncoed Centre, Cyncoed Road, Cardiff CF2 6XD. Tel: 0222 757826. Certain Bliss materials are available from: Winslow Press, Telford Road, Bicester, Oxon OX6 0TS.

Paget Gorman. The Paget Gorman signing system is used by some individuals with learning difficulties. For further information, contact: Stewart McKenna, City Lit Centre for the Deaf, Keeley Street, London WC2B 4BA. Tel 071 242 9872.

Amer-Ind. Amer-Ind is a concept-based signing system that is considered especially suitable for adults with profound learning difficulties. It originated from American Indian signs. For further information, contact: Mrs Maggie Cooper, Colchester General Hospital, Turner Road, Colchester, Essex CO4 5JL. Tel: 0206 853535.

Communication Aid Centres

Communication Aid Centres are national resource centres. Their role is to assess individuals and to recommend the most appropriate and up-to-date communication aids. It is usual practice for a speech therapist and a carer to accompany the person with a learning difficulty who has been referred.

Communication aids are expensive and are not suitable for everyone. A careful analysis of a student's language level, cognitive abilities and of the physical movements necessary to operate an aid is crucial. Funding to purchase aids is hard to obtain and many people are of necessity fund raising at least part of the cost. Individuals using communication aids should have access to them at all times. It can be devastating for a person to be able to communicate with an aid only at certain times and in particular circumstances. People need unrestricted access to their own aids at all times (whether purchased or on loan), rather than 'only on Wednesday mornings at a day centre'. Examples of communication aids include:

My Voice. This enables a person who cannot speak but who can recognise symbols to select and press a symbol on a portable concept keyboard. This activates a recorded voice to communicate a message.

Canon Communicator. The Canon Communicator is a useful device for people who can read and write but who cannot speak comprehensibly. Messages can be typed out letter by letter on this small portable device: the words emerge typed on a narrow ribbon of paper.

Developing Opportunities for Communication and Discussion

People only communicate when they have something to say. One student in Walsall's 'Learning for Living' scheme was thought incapable of speech when he was a resident in a long-stay hospital. He started talking when he moved out of the hospital, and confided to his tutor that he had not talked in hospital because he was so bored.

The tutor's dilemma is how to encourage students to communicate. In one general education group that had been meeting for several years, the students were stiff and withdrawn in their communication and co-operation with each other. The tutors decided to change the format of the two-hour session, and to begin with a half hour coffee break to allow opportunities for informal discussion and socialisation. The effect was dramatic. Students started to talk and interact with each other, and the good communication translated to the learning situation, where students started to support each other and to discuss their learning. Creating an opportunity for people to communicate and develop social skills informally paid dividends in the structured learning situation.

Activities to Develop Conversation and Discussion

Some learning activities can be designed to stimulate conversation, listening, self-expression and discussion. Below are 10 ideas for creating opportunities to develop these skills. This list is not comprehensive or exhaustive, but offers a starting point for tutors to develop their own ideas. The activities are aimed at students in a group who already have a degree of skill in communicating.

Recording students' voices on a tape recorder. This may be a new experience for some people, who have never heard themselves speak on tape before. Students may choose to say a few words — or to record their life stories.

Students interview each other on tape. This activity has led to students developing the confidence to interview a member of staff for an 'in-house' newspaper, and to students deciding to visit a local radio station.

Sound lotto. For this, sounds on pre-recorded tapes (commercially available or home-made) can be matched to pictures or photographs. This activity can be backed up by Makaton signs if appropriate. The activity develops listening skills.

Using photographs to develop descriptive skills. For example, a student can be asked to describe a photograph of an object without naming the object, while other students guess what it is. 'It's round and you eat from it' would be a plate or a dish.

'If you won £100, what would you do with it?' *This question can trigger varying reactions from students in a group, which have included: 'I'd buy a packet of salt and vinegar crisps every day';*

'I'd buy a fur coat, a chicken and a bottle of brandy. I'd sit in bed with the fur coat on, eat the chicken and drink the brandy!'

Holidays discussion. *Students and tutors can bring in pictures and holiday brochures. Students can choose a picture and say where they think it is and why they would like to go there. Even better, they can plan a real holiday or day-trip, individually or collectively.*

Current affairs discussion. *Students can bring in a photograph or picture from a magazine or newspaper to discuss.*

Hobbies or interests. *Students can bring in something related to a hobby or interest to tell the rest of the group about. One session resulted in students bringing in music tapes, English history books, pictures of Dracula and embroidery to talk to each other about.*

The 'What if?' game. *Cards are written out or drawn with a variety of scenarios which students take one at a time and react to. Cards can include a social skills element: 'What would you do if you lost your purse?'; 'What would you do if you smelt gas?'*

The group can all join in and comment on the situation.

The 'Oh' game. *(Developed by Janet Bliss and Joan Greening, directors of the Strathcona Theatre Company.) Participants sit in a circle and pass three objects around. Each has a different 'Oh' attached to it — one sad, one disappointed and one angry. As a participant receives the object, they pass it on with the appropriate* *expression of 'Oh'. The game can be developed with the same emotions/objects but with a word chosen by the students. As the game relies partly on aural cues, it can also be used with students who have a visual impairment.*

Think for yourself

What links exist or could be developed with speech therapists for: liaison in working with individual students; seeking advice on methods and materials for developing language skills?

Have staff been offered training and support to learn alternative language systems (such as Makaton or Blissymbols) where appropriate?

What resources are currently available to support the development of language and communication skills?

What new teaching materials could be usefully purchased or developed by staff?

Photographs provide a useful language teaching resource and stimulus. For what purposes could they be used?

What applications could local photographs featuring students and amenities have? Who could take them?

SUMMARY AND RECOMMENDATIONS

Various approaches can be used to develop language and communication skills.

These include structured language programmes, sign and symbol systems, communication aids and the development of opportunities for self-expression.

A communication difficulty should not exclude students from learning.

Tutors may have to learn new ways of communicating by sign or symbol in order to respond to individual needs.

Tutors should be responsive to creating opportunities for communication to take place.

RESOURCES AND FURTHER READING

Photographic teaching materials useful for developing language skills are available from: Winslow Press, Telford Road, Bicester, Oxon OX6 0TS; and from Learning Development Aids, Duke Street, Wisbech, Cambs PE13 2AE.

Further Reading

Philip Jones & Ailsa Cregan *Sign and Symbol Communication for Mentally Handicapped People.* Croom Helm, 1986.

Chris Williams *Towards Teaching Communication Skills. A model for use with the profoundly and severely handicapped.* British Institute of Mental Handicap, 1973.

Elspeth McCarthy *Helping ATC Students to Communicate.* British Institute of Mental Handicap, 1984.

Chris Kiernan, Barbara Reid & Linda Jones *Signs and Symbols.* Heinemann, 1983.

Courses on Language Development

Details are available from: The College of
Speech Therapists, Harold Poster House,
6 Lechmere Road, London NW2 5BU;
and from Castle Priory College, Thames
Street, Wallingford, Oxon OX10 0HE.

TEACHING STUDENTS WITH PROFOUND AND MULTIPLE LEARNING DIFFICULTIES

A small but growing number of people are
taking seriously the learning needs of
adults with profound and multiple
learning difficulties. Two hospital-based
case studies are described where high
quality individual work by educational
practitioners is benefiting adults who have
profound and multiple learning
difficulties. A hospital base offers few
opportunities for integration into the
outside world, and can create isolation for
staff as well as for students. To date,
education has offered little for adult
students with profound and multiple
learning difficulties. The available
provision is mostly on an outreach basis
in long stay hospitals. This scenario must
change.

With Care in the Community initiatives
developing, more people with profound
and multiple learning difficulties will be
moving to live in community settings. An
increasing number of young adults with
profound and multiple learning difficulties
already in the community are leaving
special schools with no prospect of
continuing full- or part-time education, or
of obtaining a place at a social services day
centre. Many day centres are overcrowded
and have a limited number of spaces for

people with profound and multiple
learning difficulties. Imaginative ways of
resourcing and developing learning
opportunities must be found, based on the
principles of normalisation. Examples
include:

- Service brokerage, where money is
directly assigned to individuals to
build up tailor-made programmes, is
currently being developed in certain
areas of the country.

- Lancaster University is considering
running a full-time course for young
adults with profound and multiple
learning difficulties based on the main
campus. Staff and students from the
university would be actively involved
in integrating the students into the life
of the university. Staff from a wide
range of departments, including
archaeology, history, biological
science and modern languages, have
willingly offered to devise appropriate
learning packages.

More initiatives like these are urgently
needed.

Work at Pewsey Hospital, Wiltshire

The Wyvern Special Education Centre at
Pewsey Hospital is an outreach site of
Swindon College. The centre is staffed by
three lecturers from the college, eight
part-time tutors and six teaching
assistants. One lecturer specialises in
developing work with hospital residents
who have visual impairments, who are
taught the skills of mobility. The other
two lecturers have concentrated on
students who have challenging behaviour

or profound learning difficulties. One such group is described here, together with some of the strategies that have been employed.

Phil Martin has worked with one particular group of hospital residents for three years. When the staff team decided to do a survey of the hospital residents, Phil discovered a group of women mostly in their forties who had not taken part in any activities away from the ward. Several of them had been placed at the hospital at the age of about eight. Their behaviour and physical disabilities are such that even if efforts had been made to get them to a day activity, there would have been considerable difficulties. However, as Phil and his colleagues were targeting people who had not previously had the opportunity to take part in off-ward learning activities, it was decided to see if individual programmes within the adult education block could be developed.

It has been a long, slow process, but with significant results.

Monday 19 June, 2.00pm
We go over to the ward to collect the students. Several volunteers are already there. Twenty volunteers are on a rota and help out once a month, in groups of about four at a time. They are confident and relaxed in their dealings with the students. Today we are taking five students to the education building. Three are in wheelchairs, and two can walk over slowly, though one sits down many times on the way over. The students have no expressive language. Some of them have scratches where they have mutilated themselves and have a

history of head banging. On the ward they are slumped over and uncommunicative. I feel anxious and wonder what to expect.

2.20pm
After about 10 minutes in the education room, a transformation has taken place in the students. With stimulation, they have become alert and responsive. W. has used a Pethna box for the first time by herself spontaneously. This is a very simple machine which will turn on lights, music, a fan or a vibrating cushion as a reward when the lever or other switch is moved. A volunteer works with her to encourage her to continue. A., who usually has her arms in splints to prevent her making herself sick or banging her own head, is lying on a wedge with her hands in cool water. She is laughing and smiling. L is looking up and making eye contact, holding her head up high and smiling. A volunteer is gently washing her hands and talking to her. N. has inhaled lavender, which has been found to relax her, and has had her shoulders massaged for the same reason. She is now using a tailor-made computer programme, with support. When she touches the screen, the computer plays some of her favourite music. She holds on to the table and dances from side to side.

3.00pm
The students enjoy music as a group activity, Phil plays the guitar and the volunteers join in with songs. The

students are reacting to the sounds in individual ways. Some of them move in time to the music.

Careful recording has shown the progress that students have made. The Pre-Verbal Communication Schedule (Kiernan and Reid, NFER) has proved useful in assessing the communication skills of this non-verbal group. Video recordings have shown developments in making eye contact or in learning how to walk unsupported. Regular and detailed profiles are sent to ward staff to inform them of progress made. Two examples of the assessment/review summary sheets are shown. The one to one support given by the pool of volunteers makes this highly individual level of work possible. Phil Martin is leaving the hospital to move to a new job. His main concern is whether anyone else will want to take on the special challenges of working with this particular group of students. Will they be able to continue their development, or will they once again be labelled 'ineducable'?

WYVERN SPECIAL EDUCATION CENTRE

Assessment/review summary
Student: D
Date of Test: 14.1.88
Summary Updated: 7.7.89
Test(s) Used: Pre-Verbal Communication Schedule
Copies to: Ward Speech Therapist
General remarks
D's behaviour has shown a steady improvement over the last two years,

although she still has days where she persistently head-bangs and is very unresponsive.
Summary of test results
D has well-developed preferences and enjoys a range of activities. She particularly likes music, and some types of music appeal to her more than others (she especially seems to like waltz time). D's vision is good and she picks up visual cues in a situation (e.g. tea being made). Her physical control is limited due to very high muscle tone, which interferes with her balance in walking and with use of her hands. D's hearing is good and she can tap to the beat of music. She is not able to imitate any action or sound. D communicates through non-speech noises, facial expression and behaviours such as head-banging. She reaches out to be lifted, and touches other people to get their attention.
Educational needs identified
D is unlikely to develop speech, signing or use of symbols. She needs help to develop ways of communicating which are socially acceptable (e.g. taking a person's hand, not grabbing their hair). D needs to learn to use her hands; she rarely picks anything up.
D has no comprehension of speech, but she can pick up visual cues. She therefore needs strong gestural cues and would benefit if Makaton signs were used when speaking to her.
D needs regular music (therapy) and relaxation sessions to calm her. She finds the smell of lavender particularly soothing.

D needs to learn that her actions can produce specific changes in her environment (e.g. operating a switch or touchscreen will switch on music).

Recommendations

Remain in Early Development Group at present.
Further advice to be sought re: relaxation of muscle tension.

WYVERN SPECIAL EDUCATION CENTRE

Assessment/review summary

Student: G
Date of Test: 10.2.88
Summary Updated: 7.7.89
Test(s) Used: Pre-Verbal
Communication Schedule
Copies To: Ward Speech Therapist

General remarks

G has a spinal deformity which causes her to lean to the right when sitting. She wears arm splints to prevent her from head-banging and sticking her fingers in her mouth. She has periods when she is sick constantly. Because she tends to slump over when sitting, we have found it helpful to lie her on a wedge. This makes it possible for G to use her arms (mainly for splashing in water which she enjoys). It also straightens her spine and seems to reduce head-banging and vomiting.

Summary of test results

G's vision seems good and she has developed the ability to track a moving object. However she does not for instance scan the features of someone's face when looking at them. She will turn her head towards a sound which would indicate that she is able to hear — although I understand that she has been considered deaf in the past. G can release objects from her hand but cannot reach out for objects. She will accept things in her grasp only on odd occasions. She has differential responses to smells and seems particularly to like the smell of cloves. G makes sounds which all appear to be expressing negative sensations — but this is not always the case. G can smile and now does so regularly, especially when she first comes into the room and when she is touched or held; this was an unusual occurrence only a year ago. G shows no other communication which can be considered to be intentional.

Educational needs identified

G needs to have sensory experiences brought to her, as she is unable to move to them.
A wedge has now been prescribed by the Physiotherapist specifically for G and has formed part of a programme to make her more aware of the extensor areas of her body, leading to her stretching and straightening out when lying on her back or front. She needs to be encouraged to do this or she curls up into a foetal position.
G needs to have her splints removed and her hands held and massaged. Her eye contact needs to be sought. Her smile should be encouraged and when it occurs should be interpreted as communicating 'I like this', and re-inforced accordingly.

Recommendations
Remain in Early Development
Group on Monday and Thursday
afternoons. We need continuing
advice from the physiotherapist.

Orchard Hill Further Education Centre, Sutton

'*Every individual has the right to be respected and valued as an individual, whose rights are neither changed nor diminished because they have special needs.*'
'*Every individual has the ability to learn.*'

Background. The Orchard Hill Further Education Centre is based at Queen Mary's Hospital in Carshalton, Surrey. Approximately 200 young adults with profound and multiple learning difficulties are permanent residents in one area of the hospital. The rest of the complex functions as a hospital for sick children.

The residents with learning difficulties are mostly in their twenties and thirties. They had originally been placed at The Fountain Hospital in London, which was one of two locations which took babies with severe disabilities from all over England. They were transferred to Queen Mary's Hospital between 1960 and 1964, when The Fountain Hospital was rebuilt to become St George's Hospital in Tooting. There are no plans in the short-term to move the residents into the community. All of the residents have profound learning difficulties, with most of them having a major physical disability as well. One hundred and seventy residents are confined to wheelchairs or

spinal carriages. The combination of learning difficulty and physical disability results in serious communication problems for the majority of the residents. Only 10 students out of 200 are able to speak a few words.

The National Development Team visited the hospital in 1978, and expressed concern at the lack of opportunities and facilities for the 'Fountain group', as they are still known. The Department of Health approached the Department of Education and Science for funding, which was granted and implemented in 1983. In 1989/90 Sutton LEA assumed responsibility for funding the centre.

Staffing. Freda Abbro, lecturer in charge, was appointed in 1983. The centre has since expanded from a two-person operation to employing 20 full-time staff who respond to the educational needs of the 200 residents of the unit. The centre is sited in two converted wards.

Team Work. Staff work in teams of three, which comprise a lecturer, a senior teaching aide and a teaching aide. The size of group varies according to need and activity, with some working on a one to one ratio and other groups catering for up to seven students.

Staff Development. Staff development is a key area. One afternoon a week is devoted to staff development activities. These are attended by lecturers and teaching aides, who work alongside each other to share skills and experience. This approach results in a close and tightly knit staff group, where ideas on activities and equipment are shared and support is readily available. Stress is an inevitable factor of the work, and as about 10 students a year die from degenerative diseases, bereavement and loss is a sadly regular feature of the work.

Staff Accreditation. No appropriate form of training was available for staff working with adults with profound and complex learning difficulties. In 1989 Freda Abbro and her deputy, Claire Howley, tutored a new 40-hour course which is being validated by the Regional Advisory Council for Supply, Education and Training of Teachers. All staff have completed this course, which aimed to enhance confidence and competence in working as adult educators with students who have profound and complex learning difficulties. The course participants themselves were instrumental in designing the course to suit their needs.

Centre Programme. The centre operates on an extended year basis, with groups operating for 47 weeks of the year. This continuity is essential for the retention of skills and learning. The following are key areas which are offered in six-month courses:

- communication
- motor skills
- perceptual/cognitive skills
- work with students who have visual impairment.

Nursing staff are instrumental in determining the individual learning targets, so that they will be motivated to reinforce the learning programmes devised by education tutors. Choices and decision making opportunities are built into the planning wherever possible. Learning goals are of necessity presented in small steps — for instance: 'Julie will maintain eye contact for 10 seconds in order to build on her communication skills.'

Taster courses are offered in 12-week blocks in the following areas:

- horticultural therapy
- sensory stimulation
- music, movement and drama
- social interaction
- swimming
- motor skills.

In addition, a 'Travelling Roadshow' has been very successful in taking music and sensory stimulation into residential units. It has broken down barriers between health and education staff, with staff from both areas becoming involved in eliciting reactions and responses from the students.

Principles of Learning. Freda Abbro has developed four steps for effective learning, which are clearly displayed in the teaching rooms:

First: involve the client from the beginning. Treat the client the way that you would like to be treated. Put yourself in his [sic] shoes and try to feel what he feels. The client's likes and wants should be part of each goal that is set. As much as possible, the client should participate in setting the goals. Always explain the goals to the client.

Second: use the client's strengths to set goals which help with his needs. Make a list of the client's strengths — what he can do, what he likes to do and other people who are willing to help. Make a list of his needs — possible goal areas. Review the strength list to see how his strengths can be used to help with his needs.

Third: use small steps to reach the goal. Try to make each step something you can achieve in a few days to a week. Each step should be mastered before going on to the next. If you aren't making progress, it's probably because your steps aren't small enough.

Fourth: state clearly who will do what and when. Describe what the client will do or how he will be acting when the goal is achieved. Make some person or persons responsible for helping the client achieve each step. Always have a target date for the step you are working on. (This can be changed.) Spell out clearly what is to be done so that a new person could read the plan and know what to do.

Further Information. Orchard Hill FE Centre has made a professional video of its work. For information about the video, or about the work at the centre, contact: Freda Abbro, Head of Centre, Orchard Hill FE Centre, Queen Mary's Hospital, Carshalton, Surrey SM5 4NR.

Barriers to Access for Adults with Profound and Complex Learning Difficulties

Adults who have profound and complex learning difficulties or challenging behaviour are often excluded from education provision. Barriers to access include:

Physical Barriers. For students in wheelchairs, getting access to colleges and adult education centres can be difficult. Transport is often a problem while many buildings lack suitable ramps and toilets for disabled people.

Care Needs. Students with profound and multiple learning difficulties may well need individual assistance with personal care needs. Extra staffing and adequate facilities are required to meet these needs.

Attitudinal Barriers. 'They'll never learn anyway.' 'I don't like these handicapped students cluttering up the corridors.' The attitude block can be two-way. Staff working in educational settings can be loathe to take on board students perceived as having complex and 'difficult' needs. Staff working in other agencies may refer only more able students so that the scheme is perceived as more likely to run smoothly.

Staff Development Issues. Staff need support and training in order to feel confident in working with students who have complex learning difficulties. (See Chapter 10 for a full discussion on staff development.)

Finance. Students with profound and multiple learning difficulties or challenging behaviour need high staff/student ratios. The most effective work is implemented on a one to one basis. Specialist equipment, aids and adaptations may need to be obtained and can be costly.

Think for yourself

What learning opportunities does your scheme currently offer for adults with profound and multiple learning difficulties?
What new opportunities could be developed?
How can this area of work be resourced?
What joint funding arrangements are available or could be accessed? How can support be gained from senior managers and officers for this area of work?
What rationale can be used when people argue that this area of work is an expensive waste of time?
How can professional staff involved in developing learning programmes work together and involve parents/carers in the development and reinforcement of learning?
What training and/or support could be offered to staff, parents/carers and volunteers?
What forms of inter-agency support and liaison are available to develop this area of work?
How can overlap/handover periods be arranged for staff working with students who have profound and multiple learning difficulties in order to ensure continuity of approach?
How can extended year provision be offered by education staff to ensure that students' skills are not lost during long academic holidays?

SUMMARY AND RECOMMENDATIONS

The case studies illustrate that a detailed individual approach to the principles of development and learning can be successfully employed with adults who have profound and multiple learning difficulties. The educational provision at Pewsey Hospital and Orchard Hill FE centre have points in common in terms of approach:

- detailed assessment, planning and recording methods

- use of a multi-sensory approach to include massage, aromatherapy, music, cookery and other tactile, visual and auditory experiences

- use of computers with suitable or individually adapted software

- building on choice and decision-making skills wherever possible (see also Chapter 4)

- liaison with other interested parties, such as carers, nursing staff, physiotherapists, speech therapists, non-teaching assistants and volunteers.

Education for adults with profound and multiple learning difficulties is an emerging area. Community-based opportunities for learning must be developed so that adults with profound and multiple learning difficulties can share the same right to learn as other citizens. Developments should be based on the principle of normalisation and should include a policy of integration rather than segregation.

RESOURCES AND FURTHER READING

Chris Kiernan & Barbara Reid *Pre-Verbal Communication Schedule*. NFER-Nelson, 1987.

Pethna boxes are available from: Toys for the Handicapped, 76 Barracks Road, Sandy Lane Industrial Estate, Stourport-on-Severn, Worcestershire DY13 9QB.

Brilliant Computing provide software and adaptations, some of which are suitable for adults with profound and multiple learning difficulties. Brilliant Computing, Box 142, Bradford BD3 0JN.

Interface Designs, 12 East Meads, Guildford GU2 5SP (tel: 0483 32909) provide a perspex overlay with holes cut out to fit over concept keyboard. Useful for people who work with their forearm over the board.

The Workers' Educational Association (Western District) has devised a syllabus for a 15-day course called 'Educating Adults with Profound Difficulties'. For further details, contact: Mandy Neville, Tutor Organiser, WEA (Western District), 40 Morse Road, Redfield, Bristol BS5 9LB.

Judy Cavet has completed an EC research project on leisure for people with profound and multiple learning difficulties. A summary is available from: Judy Cavet/James Hogg, Hester Adrian Research Centre, University of Manchester, Manchester M13 9PL.

Further Reading

Flo Longhorn *A Sensory Curriculum for Very Special People*. Souvenir Press, 1988.

Jan Hulsegge & Ad Vermeul *Snoezelen — Another World. A practical book of sensory experience environments*. Rompa, 1987. Rompa's catalogue, with details of Snoezelen multi-sensory installations and soft environments, is available from: Rompa, PO Box 5, Wheatbridge, Chesterfield S40 2AE. Tel: (0246) 211777.

David Brandon & Noel Towe *Free to Choose — An Introduction to Service Brokerage*. Available from: Good Impressions Publishing Ltd, Hexagon House, Surbiton Hill Road, Surbiton KT6 4TZ.

Carol Ouvry *Educating Children With Profound Handicaps*. British Institute of Mental Health, 1987.

MAKING SENSE OF THE WORLD FOR ADULTS WITH LEARNING DIFFICULTIES WHO ARE BLIND AND DEAF

Sense in the Midlands has premises in

Edgbaston, Birmingham, and was established in 1986. It offers full-time education and residential provision for 36 adults with severe learning difficulties who are blind and deaf, aged from 18 to 47. An estimated 90 per cent of the students have been affected by rubella. Many of them have spent years on the back wards of long-stay hospitals. There is a long waiting list — about 20 people have been assessed and considered suitable for a placement at Sense in the Midlands. However, despite a recent expansion, the provision is currently full to capacity. Once a place has been offered, funding must be obtained to finance the highly intensive programmes offered. Sense is a non-profit-making organisation, which offers a very high staffing ratio. In 1989/90 fees per resident were approximately £750 a week. Most students are funded by sponsorship from health districts and social services departments.

Staffing and Structure

A total of 120 care and education staff develop skills programmes under the guidance of three senior managers. Ratios vary from one to one at best, to three staff to five students at worst. Staff work in three shifts, and are expected to attend initial and in-service staff development programmes which are provided in-house.

Students

The philosophy of Sense is that all of its students can learn. It is expected that each student will work on between 15 and 30 individual objectives, which are carefully timetabled in order to allow learning of appropriate skills in the relevant situation.

Communication, self-help and household skills form the basis of learning programmes. Objectives are set at case conferences in which parents and Sense staff decide on priorities based on individual need.

Communication is of prime importance. Many of the students have exhibited challenging behaviours, such as head banging or faeces smearing, in their previous placements. Staff at Sense have found that much of this behaviour is caused by frustration at not being able to communicate. British Sign Language is taught sign by sign, with the signs being adapted to a tactile form so that they can be learnt by people who can neither see nor hear. Once the students feel that they are in a safe environment and that they can communicate, the level of anti-social behaviour drops rapidly.

The Environment: Making Sense of the World

The environment at Sense in the Midlands is designed to maximise the use of touch plus any residual vision or hearing that residents may have. Each room has a tactile symbol associated with it, which is attached to the door. These include a tennis ball for the sports hall, a flannel for the bathroom and personal symbols on the students' bedroom and locker doors. Students are able to feel where they are and to predict what is happening to them. The edges of doors and kitchen worktops are highlighted in contrasting colours so that they stand out for students with some residual vision, while carpets of different colours and textures differentiate room boundaries. The staff identify themselves to the students by always wearing or carrying an individual marker — sometimes a brooch, necklace or bracelet. They are able to say and sign their initial — 'Hello, it's V.' — and the students can touch the individual's marker. The doorbell of each flat triggers a fan and/or flashing light, so that students learn when to expect a visitor.

Activities can be predicted by the use of tactile symbols. This is individualised for each student, so that for one student riding is signalled by a riding hat, while another associates riding with feeling a miniature model of a horse.

Progress

All students at Sense have made substantial progress in their individual learning programmes. The aim is for students to become more independent by means of an intensive period of education. The first two years at Sense result in a rapid development of skills.

Although the programme is only in its third year, staff envisage that the consolidation and transfer of skills will be the main work of students spending a third and fourth year with them. Year five will be seen as preparation for a new setting. Sense is working to establish a long-stay unit, as suitable placements for people to move on to are hard to find.

> *Think for yourself*
>
> *How many people are there locally who have a learning difficulty combined with a sensory impairment?*

> *What training and support can be offered to staff who are working with these students in an educational role? What specialist advice on methods, materials and equipment is needed? Who could be approached to provide it?*

RESOURCES AND FURTHER READING

Sense produces a regular magazine, a publications list and an introductory reading leaflet. Sense can also provide details of relevant staff development courses. Contact: Sense (National organisation), The National Deaf-Blind and Rubella Association, 311 Gray's Inn Road, London WC1X 8PT. For information about Sense in the Midlands contact: Bob Snow/Virginia Mallett, Sense in the Midlands, 4 Church Road, Edgbaston, Birmingham B15 3TD.

Further Reading

Bob Snow & Helen Bradley *Making Sense of the World*. SENSE, 1986.

Teaching Blind Adults with Learning Difficulties

The RNIB has an information officer responsible for adults with multiple disabilities, who is willing to channel enquiries in the right direction within the RNIB. Contact: Gillian Levy, Information Officer, Royal National Institute for the Blind, 244 Great Portland Street, London WIN 6AA. Tel: 071 388 1266.

Teaching Deaf Adults with Learning Difficulties

The City Lit runs a two-day-a-week course in continuing education for deaf adults who have additional learning difficulties. Many students come from social services day centres. The total communication method is used, which incorporates speech, signing and writing. Makaton and British Sign Language are used. Further information can be obtained from: Stewart McKenna, Senior Lecturer in Continuing Education, The City Lit Centre for Deaf People and Speech Therapy, Keeley House, Keeley Street, London WC2.

TEACHING STUDENTS WITH CHALLENGING BEHAVIOUR

'The behaviour of people with learning difficulties can sometimes be negative. They've got more to contend with because of their disability, which makes them more frustrated.' (Ghislaine Fergar, self advocate.)

Challenging behaviour is a term that is commonly employed to describe the small number of people with learning difficulties whose behaviour is such that it 'challenges' the services or system. Challenging behaviour has been defined by the Special Development Team at the University of Kent as: 'behaviour of such an intensity, frequency or duration that the physical safety of the person or others is likely to be placed in serious jeopardy, or behaviour which is likely to seriously limit or delay access to and use of ordinary community facilities.'

A highly individual response is

necessary to plan and respond to the learning needs of adults who present challenging behaviour. Some individuals have been excluded from a range of services, including social services day centres and further education colleges. In many cases the people who are perceived as presenting the greatest problems are ultimately offered the least input and the fewest learning opportunities. Yet learning is seen as central to the development of individuals who exhibit challenging behaviour:

'Almost everyone who displays these behaviours will need some individual help or tuition in learning new acceptable behaviours or skills, or in learning coping strategies and ways of dealing with their own feelings of anger, helplessness or frustration.' (Facing the Challenge, King's Fund, 1987.)

The closure of long-stay hospitals means that the traditional answer of hospitalisation for people with challenging behaviour is no longer a viable option. Community services are slowly developing alternatives to the hospital model. *Facing the Challenge*, the seminal King's Fund paper, describes in detail some of the issues and complexities in developing community-based services for people with challenging behaviour, based on the principle of an ordinary life. Current and developing approaches emphasise a flexible way of working in whatever situations the challenging behaviour is arising. Traditionally, people were placed in special units (or 'sin bins') for a set period, but the challenging behaviour would often recur once they were back in their everyday environment.

Approaches to Challenging Behaviour

Learning to behave in a socially acceptable manner is seen as a priority in programme planning. An individual response can be developed using one or more of the following approaches.

Behaviour Modification. Behaviour modification involves the systematic and structured reward of the desired behaviour. It has been used successfully with people who have profound or severe learning difficulties. Some people have reservations about the ethics of behaviourism in controlling and shaping behaviour.

Alternative Skills Development. New skills are developed as an alternative in order to redirect energy and attention from negative or destructive acts to more creative activities. One student started to attack the escort on the social services bus to the local day centre. For a while he was transported by taxi, but this approach was expensive and did not overcome the root problem of aggression. A psychologist decided to teach some creative skills. The student learnt to draw and to discriminate between colours. He enjoyed learning the new skills, and the programme was backed up by a token economy system in which behaving appropriately resulted in a favourite drink of coke or coffee. The approach was successful, and the student started to travel on the bus again without incident.

Counselling and Psychotherapy. Giving people with challenging behaviour time and space to talk about their problems is a learning experience. Practitioners have found that this approach works well with people who are able to communicate verbally, and who would reject behaviour modification programmes. People can receive counselling in a group or one to one situation. Learning to listen and to communicate problems in a group has led to a reduction in challenging behaviour for participants.

Relaxation Sessions. Some people with challenging behaviour are highly stressed and anxious. Learning to relax is of great importance. Approaches may include yoga, music, massage, aromatherapy and breathing exercises.

Employment. The 'Intowork' scheme in Sheffield (see page 74) successfully places adults with challenging behaviour into paid employment. The experience of learning to work in a real life situation develops skills and social competence, while the challenging behaviour diminishes.

Life Story Work. Drawing together information — whether from tapes, photos, diaries, albums, letters, scrapbooks or videos — about a person's life can help to make sense of the past, and emphasises the concept of past, present and future experiences. People with learning difficulties are sometimes denied the opportunity to build a personal record of their lives. Staff can work with students to develop a life story. In the case of people with challenging behaviour, past events or goodbyes may have been painful or distressing. Compiling a positive record based on strengths and achievements, while at the same time acknowledging hurts and disappointments, can be constructive and therapeutic. It can lead to positive developments in the sense of self-worth for students. It also enables staff to empathise with the negative experiences a person with challenging behaviour may have had.

Interaction Teaching. Staff at Harperbury Hospital School have developed learning through using social interaction as a basis to develop communication skills. Adult students at a pre-verbal stage of development who are 'hard to reach' learn to interact socially. They are encouraged and stimulated by teaching staff working in teams who use interactive strategies which are sensitive to developing a reciprocal, communicating relationship.

'Gentle Teaching'. This is an American term to embrace non-aversive approaches to working with people who have challenging behaviour. It offers a person-centred approach which shuns punitive methods.

Staff Development

The Workers' Educational Association (Western District) is developing and running a 40-day course entitled 'Developing Skills and Strategies in Relation to Challenging Behaviour'. The course is aimed at professionals across agencies, parents and volunteers who are involved with people who have challenging behaviour. The course emphasises non-aversive techniques and offers participatory learning including practical work, discussion and visits. For further information contact: Mandy Neville (Tutor Organiser), WEA (Western District), 40 Morse Road, Redfield, Bristol BS5 9LB.

Think for yourself

Does provision currently cater for people described as having challenging behaviour?
If yes:
What approaches are used?
How are staff supported?
What improvements or developments could be made?
If no:
What happens to people who are excluded from provision?
Under what criteria are they excluded?
How can their learning needs be met?
What are the resource implications?

RECOMMENDATIONS

Close liaison with relatives/carers and key workers is essential to reinforce learning programmes and to monitor progress.

Advice from professionals working in other fields is necessary in planning educational programmes for many students with learning difficulties and additional complications.

Relevant colleagues may have

experience in psychology, speech therapy, physiotherapy services, or work for RNIB, RNID or Sense.

Effective recording procedures in relation to assessment, planning and evaluation are necessary to demonstrate progress.

Staff may need to work one to one or in a very small group for learning activities. The work should be accordingly resourced. The use of team tutoring, non-teaching assistants or volunteers is necessary.

Imaginative ways of working should be developed according to the principles of normalisation.

RESOURCES AND FURTHER READING

The Special Development Team at the University of Kent have supported the development of initiatives in setting up community-based services for people with challenging behaviour. In addition, the Special Development Team wrote six articles which have been published in British Institute of Mental Handicap magazines. Reprints are available. Details and annual reports are available from: The Special Development Team, Social Psychology Research Unit, Beverley Farm, The University, Canterbury, Kent CT2 7LZ.

The Tavistock Clinic offers short courses, open meetings and reading lists on psychotherapy and counselling for people with learning difficulties. Details from: The Tavistock Clinic, Child and Family Department, Tavistock Centre, 120 Belsize Lane, London NW3 5BA.

For information on interaction teaching contact: Dave Hewett, Harperbury Hospital School, Harper Lane, Radlett, Hertfordshire.

Further Reading

Roger Blunden & David Allen (eds) *Facing the Challenge: An ordinary life for people with learning difficulties and challenging behaviour*. King's Fund Centre, 1987.

J. McGee *Gentle Teaching*. Human Sciences Press, New York, 1987.

Ewa Zarkowksa & John Clements *Problem Behaviour in People with Severe Learning Disabilities*. Routledge, 1988.

H. Lovett *Cognitive Counselling and Persons with Special Needs: Adapting behavioural approaches*. Praeger, New York, 1985.

Jane Clifton *Facing the Challenge in Keighley*. Barnardos, 1989.
A project report is available from: 136 Malsis Road, Keighley, West Yorkshire BD21 1RP. Tel: 0535 600032.

CONTINUING EDUCATION FOR ADULTS WITH LEARNING DIFFICULTIES IN A SECURE ENVIRONMENT

A small proportion of people with learning difficulties are convicted of offences, or are detained in the interests of their health or safety or for the protection of others. People with learning difficulties may enter secure hospital accommodation under a section of the 1983 Mental Health Act. This results in detention on the secure wards of long stay hospitals, in regional secure units or at special hospitals such as Broadmoor, Rampton or Ashworth (formerly Park Lane and Moss Side). People with learning difficulties are sometimes convicted and enter the penal system, going into Her Majesty's Youth Custody Centres or into the adult prisons. People considered 'unfit to plead' under the 1964 Criminal Procedure (Insanity) Act can also be detained in secure accommodation under a hospital order.

The learning needs of students in locked environments are complicated by emotional and psychological difficulties. For some people, being locked away from family and friends leaves many personal problems unresolved. For others, the prime motivation to attend education classes is that it offers an alternative to being locked in a cell or on a ward.

One prison education officer, when asked if students with moderate learning difficulties used the education facilities, said that no students who could be described as having moderate learning difficulties were using the education service in the prison. The member of staff then described the level of personal organisation and skills required to get to a class, including: remembering what day the class is running; remembering what time the class is running; remembering to ask to be unlocked at the appropriate time. For people who may have difficulty in remembering, a poor concept of time or who may lack assertion skills, this process of access effectively excludes them from education.

Provision at the Mount Youth Custody Centre

The Mount is a penal establishment in Bovingdon, Hertfordshire for young male offenders aged 17 to 21 from the south of England. The education department is staffed by six full-time tutors and a variable number of part-timers, and is managed by Dacorum College in Hemel Hempstead. One of the objectives of the provision defined by Beryl Hunter, Education Officer at the Mount, is to provide a balanced programme of educational activities, ranging from Open University to Basic Education, with particular emphasis on the teaching of transferable skills.

All new 'trainees' at the prison are given a talk about the work of the education department on arrival. Options include vehicle mechanics, art and design, business studies and lifeskills. The majority of courses are full-time and operate of necessity on a roll-on, roll-off basis as the men start and finish their sentences at various times. All are given an individual education guidance interview with an experienced tutor to establish if they wish to continue their education, and to determine their learning interests and needs. A high proportion of trainees have difficulty in retaining concentration and motivation. Incidents of verbal and physical aggression flare up from time to time. Two uniformed prison officers patrol the corridors of the educational block and will respond quickly to the alarm bells sited in each room. Racial tensions occasionally surface. A high proportion of the trainees are from ethnic minority communities. Social, psychological, personal and emotional complications can interfere with the learning processes. A proportion of trainees are additionally identified as having moderate learning difficulties. A full-time general education course is available for those who wish to participate, to develop their basic skills.

The General Education Course. The general education course offers full-time education for six students with a range of learning difficulties. There is a strong emphasis on literacy, numeracy and computer aided learning. The tutor in charge employs a negotiated approach to individual programme planning, and uses the students' varied interests and motivation as a base for developing learning activities.

Regular use is made of the prison library by the group. For two sessions a week the students can choose creative options (art, woodwork, cookery) to broaden their education, and to learn alongside other students.

The education sessions are long, from 9 to 11.15 in the mornings and from 2 to 4.30 in the afternoons. This is dependent on unlocking times and no flexibility is possible. Tutors working in the prison have to devise ways of breaking the sessions into short, varied activities to retain interest.

'The general education group is small today. There are two regular students and a third who was not expected and was not due to join the group. However, he has stayed since it is not possible for him to be escorted back

to his house unit. The group is reading a Spirals play about a bungled post office raid. It is very funny, and tutors, students and visitor alike all enjoy the humour. Afterwards, the students work on a computerised game of Hangman which they are writing themselves. One of the clues is: Men and women enjoy ... The answer is sex.'

Issues of sex education and AIDS education are met head-on by prison education staff, with help from outside specialists. The use of condoms is shown on a demonstration model. General education students receive these sessions alongside other students.

When people leave prison, the education staff provide contacts in the community so that students can continue their education if they choose to.

Think for yourself

List secure environments that exist locally or regionally. This may include hospitals, secure units, prisons and youth custody centres.
Whose responsibility is it to ensure that adequate learning opportunities are available in these different situations?
Are people with learning difficulties resident in these establishments?
How can their educational needs be addressed in an appropriate way?

Adult Education for Residents of the Secure Unit at Little Plumstead Hospital, Norfolk

Little Plumstead Hospital is a long-stay hospital for people with learning difficulties, which is located in rural Norfolk. Adult education work started on a small scale at the hospital in 1983. In 1986, a purpose built adult education centre was opened. The centre is the result of joint working between the health service and the education department. It is totally funded by the district health authority, and managed on an agency basis by the area head of adult education for central Norfolk. The work is steered by a multi-disciplinary policy group, whose members include hospital and education managers, psychiatrists and representatives from occupational therapy, psychology, patient care, the nurse training school, Norwich City College and social services.

Seventy-five students attend the centre twice-weekly. By negotiation with health staff, the education provision is targeted at two distinct groups — people with profound and multiple learning difficulties and people from the secure unit. The adult education centre is staffed by a co-ordinator, five tutors and five non-teaching assistants.

Thirty residents of the Secure Unit receive education either at the hospital's adult education centre or on the wards. Education is offered on the wards for students without ground parole.

Work at the adult education centre is student-centred. This approach has been used successfully with the students from the secure unit. Students assess themselves and set their own objectives. The tutor, Sue Cowan, comments that: 'Students set personal objectives so that the curriculum is seen to be their own choice and therefore relevant to them, rather than a programme imposed upon them.'

Students from the secure unit are referred to adult education for various reasons, including rehabilitation, confidence-building and in order to develop independence. Their expectations may be low, but students have their perceptions changed when they discover that adult education:

- can be fun

- leads to the development of new knowledge and skills

- fosters feelings of personal success and respect from others

- offers the benefits of learning in a group.

Students have developed social skills in terms of conversation, negotiation and assertiveness. Problem-solving is an important feature of the work.

Sue Cowan has found particular constraints in working with students from the secure unit. Difficulties experienced or presented by students include severe mental illness, challenging behaviour, mental blocks and panic attacks. Some students lack motivation or find it hard to concentrate, while others have a poor self-image. Sue takes the view that each individual has the potential for self-development. She describes this as a humanistic approach, based on the work of Carl Rogers, which seeks to develop self-reliance. The following case study demonstrates the way in which students are involved in their own learning.

David Smith (not his real name) carried out his own self-assessment with a tutor, which shows the developments he has made in basic skills.

Literacy: David can now read. He says that he could not read before. The significant point is that he has the self-esteem now to say he can read and that it is important to him. David says his spelling has improved. This is borne out by the tutor. When asked why spelling is important to him, he replied 'because I am able to write my Mum letters.' He can now write a diary freehand, with no help: 'It helps to pass the time away.' (As he has no ground parole and cannot walk around the grounds unaccompanied, this is not a frivolous comment.)

Numeracy: David is able to read and work through the money cards on his own. He has grasped equivalent values of money and is looking forward to progressing on to more difficult money and budgeting sums. He now has the confidence to select his own education work from the resources and he scans the books to find appropriate materials.

David is very highly motivated towards improving his education skills. He spends a great deal of his own time doing extra work in the evenings.

SUMMARY AND RECOMMENDATIONS

Access to education should be available, and should not depend on a high level of personal skills in order to access the available opportunities.

This has implications for:

Presentation of information. The use of video or photographs should be considered as an alternative to written material describing learning opportunities. Counselling and personal interviews are more effective than giving questionnaires for completion to people who may have limited literacy.

Getting to and from education groups. Students with learning difficulties may need extra support in achieving attendance.

Support in the learning situation. Depending on the individual and the learning situation, students with learning difficulties may require additional support in terms of staffing or adapted materials.

FURTHER READING

Anne Leonard (ed.) *An Ordinary Life and Treatment Under Security for People with Mental Handicap.* King's Fund Centre, 1990.

8. Transition to community living

'I never want to go back to that hospital to live again. No, never.' (Susan James, adult education student.)
'I felt a bit sorry. I felt how lucky I was to be living at home.'
'I felt it was sad to see people in there. They could have a normal life in the community.'
'I wouldn't like to live there.'
'There's no shops out there. It's nowhere near town. It's miles from anywhere.'
'A lot of the people could live in a group home and have an ordinary life.' (Comments from self advocates following a visit to a long-stay hospital.)

In 1989 an estimated 31,555 people with learning difficulties were still resident in long-stay hospitals in England and Wales. (Statistics from *Caring for People*, the 1989 White Paper.)

The hospitalisation of people who are not ill has been seen as an anachronism for the past 20 years. In *Caring for People*, the government states its intention to develop 'new forms of service' on an inter-agency basis in order that people with learning difficulties 'should only be in NHS facilities when they have medical or nursing needs which cannot practicably be met other than in such facilities.'

Ideas and policy have developed faster than practice in most areas. It is widely accepted that the 'medical model' of hospitalising people with learning difficulties is inappropriate for their needs and rights. Thousands of people are still resident in large hospitals, denied as yet the opportunity to live in the community.

The gradual run down and closure of long-stay hospitals under the care in the community policy requires an appropriate response by staff working in an educational role with adults who have learning difficulties. *Care and Education in the Community* by Peter Lavender (FEU/Longman, 1988) examines the implications of community care initiatives for further and adult education providers. It describes relevant legislation, planning structures, and joint finance procedures. Research by NIACE (*Care in the Community: Adult continuing education and joint finance*, 1987) found that education was frequently not represented at joint care planning meetings, or was represented by a person without a specialist knowledge of the education of adults.

Caring for People, the government White Paper which followed the Griffiths Report, assigns responsibility for community care to local authorities, who are expected to produce and publish development plans and to make 'maximum use of the independent sector'. By implication, a growth in the use of voluntary and private homes is certain. The role of education in relation to *Caring for People* is addressed by Peter Lavender in a series of articles in *Adults Learning* (February and March 1990). Lavender sees a clear role for local education authorities in two areas: direct provision for adults with special educational needs in relation to community care initiatives, and staff development via the further and higher education sector.

This chapter addresses some of the issues relating to education and community care for people with learning difficulties. It looks at ways in which learning can enable people to make the transition to a more independent life in the community.

Topics considered in this chapter are:

- The role of education for people currently in long-stay hospitals and in relation to the preparation, transition and support of people moving from institutions to the community. This section is in two parts — 'Central Issues' and 'Theory into Practice'.

- Learning to adjust and cope in new surroundings. This is relevant for people moving out of family homes and local authority hostels, as well as from hospitals.

- Informal learning opportunities in the context of private homes which cater for people moving out from long-stay hospitals. It is anticipated that there will be a growth in private sector accommodation.

- Learning opportunities offered by a voluntary group's accommodation project for people with moderate learning difficulties.

CENTRAL ISSUES

- Education can make a significant contribution to care in the community initiatives.

- Education offers a means of maintaining and developing skills.

- Learning plays a significant role in the processes of preparation and adaptation to change.

- Learning about communication, self advocacy and decision making can help students who have been institutionalised to be more independent — whether choosing where to live or making day to day choices. An adequate level of funding is necessary to enable effective work to take place.

Funding

Funding may come from a variety of sources. In some areas, local education authorities have taken responsibility for funding continuing education for residents of long-stay hospitals. In other areas (for example Lancashire, Bedfordshire, Southwark and Newham) joint finance has been used to fund full-time education posts in hospitals or in the community. In Norfolk, adult education work at Little Plumstead Hospital is wholly funded by the health authority, but is managed by the adult education service.

Learning Options

Careful consideration must be given to the development of appropriate learning options for adults with learning difficulties who have become institutionalised over many years. Learning to communicate, to develop interpersonal skills and to make choices are of great importance. Learning to overcome challenging behaviours (see Chapter 7) may be a goal for some students. A Further Education Unit project at Hales Hospital in Norfolk is examining the development of an appropriate curriculum for people leaving long-stay hospitals.

Staff Support

Support for staff is crucial. Tutors working in long-stay hospitals can feel very isolated: 'We're miles away from the college in every sense— geographically, conceptually and philosophically.' Hospital-based education tutors may not fit neatly into health service structures, and may also be remote from education colleagues, both geographically and in terms of the work they do.

Appropriate structures must be developed to ensure that education staff working in long-stay hospitals receive adequate support in their work.

Targeting Provision

Provision must be targeted effectively with a clear focus. It is important to be clear about who the education service is serving in the hospital and why. These priorities vary according to need:

- At Little Plumstead Hospital in Norfolk, tutors, by agreement with clinical and nursing staff, concentrate on teaching adults who have profound and multiple learning difficulties, and adults on the secure wards.

- At Harperbury Hospital in

Hertfordshire, education staff work with adults who have challenging behaviours, many of whom have no other possibility to leave the ward.

Problems of Continuity and Communication

'One Monday, John didn't show up for his adult education class. When we phoned the ward, we were told that he'd left the hospital at the weekend. We didn't know he was going — couldn't say goodbye — and couldn't pass details of his work to anyone.'

Bridging the Gap

Education staff in hospitals are frequently unaware of residents moving out, as indicated above, in which case any help with preparation or transition is impossible. Various schemes are seeking to redress this situation:

- In Walsall's 'Learning for Living' scheme, the adult education co-ordinator will be taking part in hospital reviews to ensure that adult education is actively involved in individual plans for preparation and transfer to community living.

- Adult education staff at Prudhoe Hospital in Northumberland offer courses on social skills and community awareness in the geographical areas to which small groups of residents are moving.

- At Bromham Hospital in Bedford, an adult education tutor is working alongside a psychologist, an occupational therapist and nursing staff in developing transition programmes for a group of five residents who are moving out. Regular visits to the house and area to which people will be moving have been made. The gradual progress on the readiness of the house has been recorded by video and photographs. The students have helped with bricklaying and plastering, and feel it is very much 'their house'. Individual booklets kept by students record their personal choices of bedroom, wallpaper, carpets and accessories.

- Surrey Local Education Authority has four area teams of 16 full- and numerous part-time adult education tutors working in the county's four long-stay hospitals for adults with learning difficulties. The work is supported by eight non-teaching assistants and four part-time clerical staff. The teams are well resourced, and have equipment which ranges from computers to microwave ovens. Each team has its own minibus, which is important, as the hospitals are isolated and remote from good public transport routes. The curriculum includes options on self advocacy, sexuality and the Open University 'Working Together' course (P555M). The education tutors have linked up with community-based adult education institutes to help in the transition process for residents leaving hospital. The long-term aim is for the tutors to move out gradually with the residents.

Multi-Agency Working

Liaison and co-ordination across agencies is vital to save duplication, to ensure a coherent delivery of services, and to reinforce learning programmes. Tutors must where possible:

- attend and contribute to multi-agency meetings and reviews

- ensure that learning carries over into everyday situations to be reinforced by other people. This avoids learning taking place in an academic vacuum, and maximises consolidation of learning. For example, there is little point in teaching a student to sign in Makaton, to make choices or to make a cup of tea if the skills cannot be used/reinforced in other settings

For students who cannot communicate, a diary filled in by staff on his/her behalf offers an effective means of keeping in touch with what the student has been learning or doing.

Think for yourself

What role does education have both within local long-stay hospitals and in facilitating the transfer of residents to the community?
What role does the local education authority play in joint care planning?
How can better communication between staff working for different agencies be developed? Think of three ways in which your local situation could be improved.

> *In what ways can education staff working in hospitals help to bridge the gap for residents moving to live in the community?*
> *How can education staff contribute to clinical team meetings/ward meetings/case reviews?*

THEORY INTO PRACTICE

These case studies describe the contribution of adult education staff in various community care initiatives.

Putting Theory into Practice 1: From Ward F4 to Dunstable

'We used to have to sleep in a big room with the light on at the hospital. Here we can put the light out when we want, and sleep in the dark.'

The National Development Team visited Fairfield Hospital in Hertfordshire, a psychiatric hospital, in 1986. They made recommendations that a group of approximately 20 elderly men with learning difficulties, who had been inappropriately placed there in the late 1960s, should be transferred to a community setting. In 1989 some of the men were given the option of moving to Greenacre, a new community-based facility for elderly people in Dunstable. Adult education staff from Special Adult Learning Programmes in South Bedfordshire have contributed positively to this development in a number of ways:

- getting to know the men in the hospital setting to help identify their needs

- helping to develop a strengths/needs assessment format in which the men could advocate for themselves where possible

- planning and implementing a programme of visits and discussion, with video and photographic visual back up, to help the men decide whether they wanted to move out

- planning and implementing an orientation programme for the group who moved out to facilitate the learning of skills necessary for adjustment to the new surroundings at Greenacre

- through exposure to a diverse range of activities followed up by discussion, helping the men to make individual informed choices about what to do with their time as an alternative to the traditional day care model.

The orientation period included learning the way around the building and the way to nearby shops. Handling personal money was a new experience — as was choosing what to wear, serving oneself food and sleeping in a single room. Within a month, people had mastered the art of making tea and coffee. They progressed to making hot drinks without prompting — and from that stage to spontaneously offering visitors a cup of tea.

Eight out of the nine men chose not to go to the local social services day centre. Instead their time is self directed. One person has joined an art class. Another has learnt the bus journey to the library and is a regular visitor there to select books on gardening and flowers. Indoor bowls, swimming, cookery, music and horse riding are being learnt by some of the group. Two people who did not speak before have started talking, one in single words and one in sentences. One person chose to retrace his roots and re-visited the village where he grew up and worked on a farm. One of the adult education tutors commented: 'Their lifestyle has been transformed.'

These outcomes have been achieved by close collaboration between adult education staff and staff from health and social services.

Think for yourself

How can education tutors be involved in developing transition programmes?
What learning opportunities are available for people with learning difficulties who have moved from a hospital to live more independently in the community?

Putting Theory into Practice 2: Education and Community Care in Lancashire

A. The Lancaster Place Education Project

In January 1987, a joint financed education post was initiated at Blackburn College. The tutor worked with five young men in their early twenties, who had moved into a home in the community after spending most of their lives at Brockhall Hospital. The men had severe learning difficulties and a range of additional complications — from communication difficulties to visual impairment.

It was considered a priority to give the men a period of full-time continuing education. A course was designed to access facilities at the local college. The group home staff were actively involved with education staff to ensure that learning was consolidated and generalised.

A model was developed as follows:

- A home based period with visits into the local community and to the college.

- An intensive full-time phase at college in a discrete group. Taster sessions were arranged and access to wide range of college facilities was possible.

- Integration into other groups and activities at the college.

- Attendance at part-time adult classes with support as required.

At the end of the year's full-time period at college, the five students had made strides in their personal development, and were: better able to communicate — either verbally or by Makaton; more relaxed, confident and socially aware; more alert, less passive and less institutionalised; physically fitter; more independent, both at college and in the community.

A report has been published which evaluates the quality of life of the men and makes reference to the college course: *44 Lancaster Place: A Story of Resettlement* (1990, King's Fund Centre).

Think for yourself

How can opportunities at colleges and adult education centres be developed for people leaving long-stay hospitals?

B. Education in the Community for Adults with Profound and Multiple Learning Difficulties

Alison Fairhurst, a tutor in Lancashire, combines care in the community for adults with profound and multiple learning difficulties with staff development across agencies. Alison works in a health/education services funded post at Skelmersdale College with back up from a non-teaching assistant. She is able to work flexibly, and adjusts her timetable from week to week according to need. Her brief includes:

- enabling ex-hospital residents with profound and multiple learning difficulties to learn to adjust to life in a community setting

- offering staff development to health authority staff working with such people in group homes, to help implement individual learning programmes

- offering consultations to social services day centre staff about developing learning programmes for people with profound and multiple learning difficulties

- developing ways of working with people with profound and multiple learning difficulties using computers, light, sound and general stimulation

- providing sessions at the mainstream setting of Skelmersdale College for some of the 18 students she works with personally on a one to one basis

- maintaining levels of responsiveness and alertness in students.

Alison describes how her students had an enforced break in their education when the hospital school shut down. Going back after a period of four years, she found a marked deterioration in the personal skills of the group. There had been a major regression in the interactive abilities of the students. Alison commented that 'they had gone glassy-eyed and empty, like paper cut-outs.' To redress this situation, an intensive period of re-learning former skills was essential. Alison described how the students gradually came to life again after a few months of revision of skills. She is convinced that education for people with profound and multiple learning difficulties is valid because it stops deterioration of skills. 'The extra we give them is what we stop them losing.'

Think for yourself

How can the educational needs of adults with profound and multiple learning difficulties who are transferring to the community be assessed and responded to?

Putting Theory into Practice 3: Communication Skills for People with Little or no Speech

The adult education service in Devon offers provision for people with very severe communication difficulties who have left hospital to live in group homes. It was decided to offer a 10-week pilot course for people who had moved into the community, with support workers or volunteers acting as their individual study partners. The course aimed to develop communication skills through the use of Makaton sign language (see Chapter 7). The students with learning difficulties and their study partners both learnt to sign together, and practised between sessions to reinforce learning. Friendships developed as students, staff and volunteers worked together. The course was held once weekly at a community college in Teignmouth.

The pilot course proved so successful that the scheme is expanding to Exeter and it is planned to make the scheme county-wide, eventually.

Think for yourself

How can the learning needs of people without speech be met in a community setting?
How can learning in the community contribute to the move from hospital to 'an ordinary life'?

LEARNING TO ADJUST AND COPE IN NEW SURROUNDINGS

'It's coming to this class that's kept me going since I've been on my own. I didn't need the social workers or anything.' (Adult education student.)

Moving from a Family Home or Hostel to Live Independently

The care in the community policy has focused attention on the move to the community for residents of long-stay hospitals. The move to independent community living is also a step that is made by people with learning difficulties who have been living with family or in hostels. The desire to learn appropriate skills and strategies to cope independently is a feature common to people moving to live in the community, whether from a hospital, family home or local authority hostel. *Letting Go* (Richardson and Ritchie) examines the complexity of parental responses to the idea of their adult son or daughter with a learning difficulty leaving home.

The Challenges of Moving to a Group Home

Hazel Ratcliff talked about her experiences of learning in relation to moving to a group home, which has 'minimal support' from staff.

Getting started. 'It's a big step. I started very slowly — I didn't know how I'd react. But look at me now! It's all changed. Doing your own independence and that — like doing *your own ironing, washing, your own bed.'*

Learning to use buses. *'It was very hard to get used to going on the bus. I feel more confident to go on the bus on my own now. You can get buses — go into town — have your friends round. I miss my mum sometimes. I have to get two buses to go and see her.'*

Learning around the house. *'We learnt to do beds and cleaning and washing. I've got a lot to learn yet. It's very slow. When I used to be at home mum used to make my bed. Now I have to get my finger out and do it for myself! My own life is all different now. Now I've got a chance to get in that kitchen and do something for myself. I didn't do that before — not at all. I'm getting used to doing what I want to do now. I can have my dinner what time I like. I'm a spaghetti bolognaise person!'*

Learning about money. *'I do my own post office work. I put my money in and take it out with my book. I'm still learning about using money — help with bills — how much they are.'*

Leisure time and adult education. *'I go out a lot — yoga — two clubs when I've got the time. I won a darts trophy in Watford. Sometimes I go and see my mum. I go to a yoga evening class. It's relaxing — I'll give you that! It's fun. I like meeting different people. I go to another class on Wednesday to get a bit more help in learning to read and write, and about using money. I feel I can speak up for what I want now. Now I'm*

independent I'm a different person.'

Finding Flexible Strategies

A group of Midlands-based social services instructors discussed their role in teaching people with learning difficulties to prepare for independent living in group homes. The majority of the people they work with live in family homes or hostels, and hope to move to group homes in the near future. A training house in the community provides a base for the project.

Confidence-building is seen as crucial to the development of independence. The staff reject a purely skills-based model on the basis that self confidence must be established in order to learn effectively. The tutors get to know the students gradually and offer sessions on a one to one basis, in which students plan activities of their choice, carried out with support if needed. This can be quite informal — such as going for a coffee or to a garden centre — and often provides a chance for the student to talk through personal feelings about being more independent and leaving home.

'Learning to make choices opens up the world for people', commented one tutor. 'At first, just choosing between tea or coffee can be a fundamental decision.' Decision-making, confidence and skills develop as students make progress in their individual and group programmes. Teaching strategies are flexible, according to the student's needs. Staff are adamant that assessment should be a tool for use rather than an end in itself. Task analysis has proved helpful. 'It also helps to try things out yourself. A lot of the teaching is physical, gestural and non-verbal. It helps if you understand how you learn, observe how the students learn, and try to minimise failure. If the staff haven't thought it through properly, the students are doomed to failure, through no fault of their own ...'

Staff face many dilemmas.

'We try to encourage self advocacy. Sometimes students end up in a big individual programme plan meeting and the goal planning is done for them. We're trying to change that.'

'Which should be ready first — the bricks and mortar of group homes or the people preparing to live in them? We don't want to push people in before they can cope. Neither do managers want houses lying empty.'

'It's not clear what level of ongoing support will be provided once people have moved.'

'What with the White Paper, there's talk of efficiency monitoring in our work. What impact will that have on the privacy of the students?'

'People with more severe disabilities are wanting to use our services. We'll have to adapt our skills — learn Makaton — consider physical access.'

Think for yourself

What learning opportunities are currently available for adults with learning difficulties resident in family homes or hostels who want to prepare for a more independent lifestyle? How can courses be developed to cater for the needs of this group of potential students? Who would need to be involved? What resources would be needed?

Self advocacy and informed choices are key concepts in the transition to an independent lifestyle. How can learning initiatives support personal development in these areas? How can learning initiatives support staff and relatives in adjusting to change and transition?

LEARNING TO MAKE LINKS IN THE COMMUNITY

Moving to a house or flat is not in itself enough. It is the building of links and friendships within the community that forms a vital part of belonging to a neighbourhood. Relevant learning experiences include:

- learning about friendships and relationships
- learning to socialise
- learning to use leisure facilities
- joining an adult education group in the community
- learning to find one's way around the new locality (see also Chapter 5 on learning for a purpose).

Learning about Everyday Experiences

'Oh, look, they've got tomatoes in here. And are those potatoes over there?' (Hospital resident aged 68 on his first visit to supermarket.)

People who have been in long-stay hospitals or institutionalised hostels for some time are removed from everyday experiences and choices. In hospital, meals usually come ready prepared on a trolley and tea may come with both milk and sugar already mixed in. Students may need to develop interpersonal skills in a range of areas:

- developing choices

- making decisions

- self-awareness and self-confidence

- socialising

- listening

- speaking up for themselves.

A number of everyday activities may be new experiences for people learning to live more independently, for example:

- preparing food

- using public transport

- crossing a road

- going shopping

- handling money and budgeting (some students may need to learn about decimal money rather than shillings and half-crowns).

Student interest and tutor imagination and expertise can, of course, extend learning options beyond basic social and life skills.

Nic Briggs, a tutor at Prudhoe Hospital, noticed that many of his students had poor co-ordination. He wondered if ski-ing would provide an enjoyable way of improving gross

motor co-ordination and mobility. As a result, there is now an enthusiastic ski-ing group which makes regular use of the local dry ski slope. Students are much more aware and confident about their co-ordination both on the ski slope and off it.

INFORMAL LEARNING OPPORTUNITIES

Taking Risks and Taking Responsibility

In May 1989, a private home opened in Norfolk for people moving out of long-stay hospitals. The seven residents had all spent many years in long-stay institutions. For the manager, the main task was to provide opportunities for the residents to start thinking for themselves. For years in the institutions they had received orders and instructions, which had made them passive and dependent on other people. In hospital, choices and opportunities were restricted.

The residents now organise their own home with minimal assistance from staff. They do domestic chores in their own time and way, rather than being told what to do, when and how. There is a choice of food and drink, as opposed to the hospitals' measured-out allocations. The manager described the delight and bewilderment of the residents at Christmas on having such a wide choice of fruit, nuts, sweets and drinks to help themselves to.

Two of the group go out regularly to an adult education evening class to improve their literacy skills. They have also learnt to make a complicated journey by public transport to their day centre. Risk-taking is considered essential by the manager, because people need a chance to prove themselves. He describes the staff's feeling of being on tenterhooks when sending people out alone for the first time, and compares it to the anxiety experienced by parents when their children go off to tackle a new experience alone. The risks are carefully monitored, and staff have discreetly shadowed people crossing roads or making journeys alone for the first time.

The people in the group at first clung to ways of behaving which had been acceptable in the hospital context, for instance three men holding hands in a row when going out. With encouragement, they have learnt to walk independently, without clutching each other. They subsequently went to the East of England agricultural show, which is large and bustling, and successfully looked around unaccompanied all day, meeting staff only for lunch and tea.

The residents have developed and changed to such an extent that people who knew them in the hospitals scarcely recognise them any more. 'I never taught them' said the manager. 'I gave them the chance to show they had capability.'

Adapting to Village Life

At another private home in a small village in Norfolk, the manager talked about the role that informal learning plays for the nine people who live there.

The majority of the residents moved from long-stay hospitals to live in the home when it opened in 1984. Most of the residents were very institutionalised, and

some had additional erratic behaviour patterns. They have overcome these difficulties to adapt successfully to a new lifestyle. The philosophy of care is that people should live an ordinary lifestyle. Residents choose their own meals and write choices on a menu board, which helps to develop and maintain literacy skills. Everybody is involved in household tasks — from cooking and cleaning to keeping bedrooms tidy. Residents learn to do this with graduated support from the care assistants. Skills are taught in the context of normal everyday activities, rather than in isolation. Trips out into the local community are encouraged, and staff have taught one woman to make her own way into college by bus. She has yet to gain confidence to make the return trip alone — the staff are working on this.

People at the home are accepted by the local community. The manager feels that their central location (opposite the post office) has helped. Also, residents go out in ones or twos rather than *en masse*, which makes social integration much easier. The local church has been welcoming, and people living in the home were able to contribute poetry and songs to a recent carol concert. The community presence and contribution of the residents has been a learning experience for the general public, who soon realised these people were not 'murderers and rapists', as some had apparently feared.

Think for yourself

How can links be developed between private homes and the adult education service?

How can private homes ensure that informal learning opportunities are provided?

How can self advocacy be developed for residents in private homes and group homes?

LEARNING OPPORTUNITIES IN AN ACCOMMODATION PROJECT

The Rathbone Accommodation Project in Leicester eases the transition to independent living in the community for young adults with moderate learning difficulties. The project transformed the shell of an Edwardian house into three self-contained flats, which can accommodate a total of six people. Residents can stay for a period of up to two years to develop their domestic and coping skills. Developing the ability to establish good relationships is central to the aims of the project.

Individual programmes are negotiated with a key worker, and change constantly as new skills are acquired.

Since the project began in September 1987, 10 people have developed to the point of feeling confident enough to branch out on their own and to live in flats designed for single people which are provided by a housing association. The flats are in the same neighbourhood as the project, which means that people who have left can drop in if they want to. Ongoing support is offered to all those who have left.

A management team involves the Rathbone Society, the housing association and the social services department. An important decision was made to opt for flats in the main house rather than an institutional hostel. To be registered as a 'care home' would present less of a financial struggle, but would have been more remote from the reality of developing an independent lifestyle.

Anna is a black woman now in her early thirties. She grew up in local authority care. Anna's physical disability combined with a speech difficulty resulted in her being labelled as having severe learning difficulties. She went to a school for children with severe learning difficulties, and on to a traditional social services day centre. There, a social worker recognised her potential and referred her to the Leicester Rathbone Society. Anna came to the Accommodation Project inexperienced at cooking, shopping, budgeting and washing. Minor adaptations to the kitchen minimised her disability. Soon she was extremely competent in domestic skills and started making and selling banana cakes! During the daytime she attended a Rathbone Employment Training course in office skills. She was offered a job, but chose instead to spend time in her new home with her boyfriend.

Think for yourself

People with moderate learning difficulties are in many areas

considered to be beyond the remit of the care in the community policy, and of the Disabled Persons Act.
Where does this leave people like Anna, and ventures like the Leicester Rathbone Accommodation Project? What facilities and learning opportunities are available for people with moderate learning difficulties in your local area?
Could the situation be improved, and if so, how?

RECOMMENDATIONS

Adult education has a key role in teaching/supporting self advocacy skills and promoting choice for adults who are moving from one style of accommodation or provision to another.

Adult education should be a partner in designing and implementing transfer, orientation and follow-up learning programmes for people with learning difficulties moving from institutions to community living.

Steps should be taken to continue existing hospital-based adult education provision into the community at the time of a resident or residents moving out. This may require additional staff or more flexible working arrangements.

Better communication is necessary between the agencies concerned so that all parties know when and where a hospital or hostel resident is moving, and what learning support will be required.

Consideration must be given to developing a responsiveness to the changing learning needs of parents/carers and staff.

FURTHER READING AND RESOURCES

Peter Lavender *Care and Education in the Community. Special Needs Occasional Paper No 6.* Longman for the Further Education Unit, 1988.

Ann Richardson & Jane Ritchie *Letting Go. Dilemmas for parents whose son or daughter has a mental handicap.* Open University Press, 1989.

Margaret Flynn *Independent Living for Adults with Mental Handicap: A place of my own.* Cassell, 1989.

Dorothy Atkinson & Linda Ward *A Part of the Community: Social integration and neighbourhood networks. Talking Points No 3.* Values Into Action, 1986.

Sir Roy Griffiths *Community Care: Agenda for action.* HMSO, 1988.

Caring for People: Community care in the next decade and beyond. HMSO, 1989.

Alan Charnley, Veronica McGivney & Alexandra Withnall *Care in the Community: Adult continuing education and joint finance.* NIACE, 1987.

Roy McConkey *Who Cares?* Souvenir Press, 1987.

Alison Wertheimer (ed.) *Building on Positives. Staff development in community services.* King's Fund Centre, 1989.

Bringing People Back Home. Eight

videos from the South East Thames
Regional Health Authority and the
University of Kent (1987—1990).
Available from: Outset Publishing, Unit
8, Moorhurst Road, Conqueror Industrial
Estate, St Leonards-on-Sea, East Sussex
TN38 9NA.

What is Community Care? is a 12-page
pamphlet, published by Values Into
Action.

For more information on the Rathbone
Society, contact: The Rathbone Society,
Head Office, First Floor, Princess House,
Manchester M1 6DD.

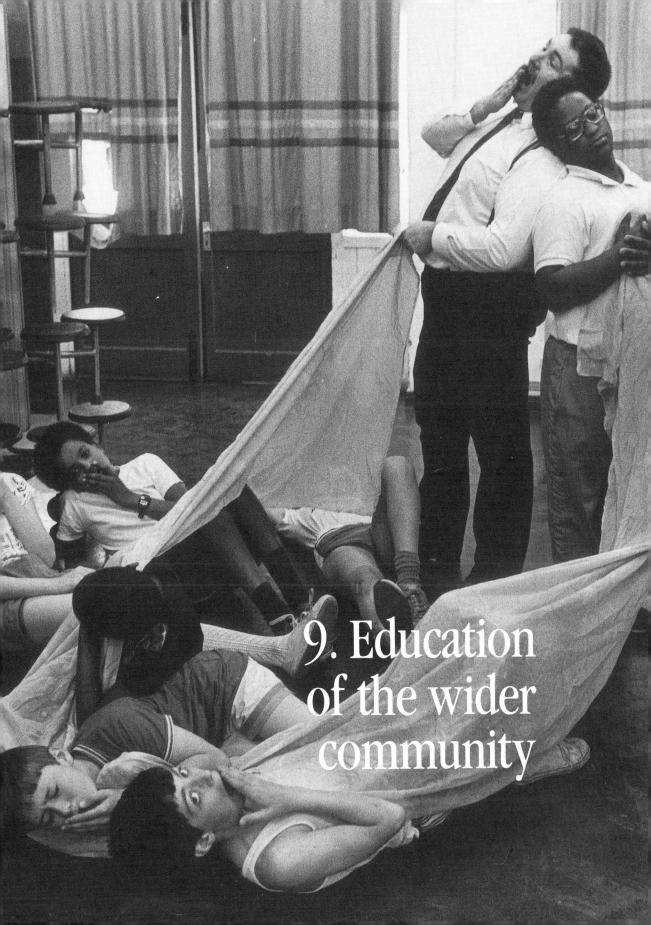

9. Education of the wider community

*'Children spit at us and call us
names. It's not nice.'*
*'People call me mental in the street.
It makes me feel terrible.'*
*'We have a lot to give. People are
beginning to realise that and to treat
us equally and like normal people.
The public should be more aware.'*
(Mark Biddle, Patsy Trott, Ghislaine
Fergar: all self advocates with
learning difficulties.)

Integration into society is a two-way
process. People with learning difficulties
who have grown up in the community
face everyday prejudice and
discrimination, as the above comments
reveal. People moving from long-stay
hospitals into the community face
opposition from groups who don't want
'them' as neighbours. This tension is
compounded by the sometimes
sensational attention of the media.

Myths about people with learning
difficulties being mentally ill, dangerous
or violent abound. People mistakenly fear
for their children, the value of their
property and the threat to their lifestyle.
One person opposing the opening of a
group home was heard to say indignantly
'But we have cats here.' What she
expected her new neighbours with
learning difficulties to do to her cats was
far from clear.

Various reports and books from
Warnock (1978) to Sines (1988) have
stressed the need for public education in
relation to issues about people with
learning difficulties and their acceptance in
the community. Research by MENCAP
has shown that a high proportion of

people still confuse learning difficulties
with mental illness. Alison Wertheimer's
review of 1,500 newspapers for Values
Into Action found that much negative
imagery was used in relation to people
with learning difficulties, described in one
report as 'the more unfortunate of God's
creatures.' Negative media and advertising
images feed and reinforce the rejecting
attitudes harboured by some misinformed
individuals. The negative attitudes and
ostracising behaviour of some members of
society in relation to people with learning
difficulties is a matter of serious concern.
People with learning difficulties have
citizens' rights, and these rights must be
respected.

The position of NIACE as an equal
opportunities organisation is that
alongside education about race and
gender, there should be opportunities for
learning about disability. What is
currently happening and what can be
done? The issue is a fraught and sensitive
one. Some parents and professionals feel
that a 'quietly, quietly' approach is the
best way to effect change. 'People chatting
over the garden fence' is the low-key
model that some people advocate. Others,
like Roy McConkey (*Breaking Barriers*,
1983), feel that short courses have a part
to play in developing attitude change.
Many people feel uncomfortable about the
idea of one group in the community
running courses 'about' another group of
people. The active and positive
involvement of people with learning
difficulties themselves in a range of
community activities is the best way to
break stereotyped ideas about 'what
people are like' and what they can achieve.

Ill-informed views, such as: 'Of course, they all love music, don't they?', and 'They'll never learn anything, will they? So what's the point of teaching them?', are all too prevalent.

LONDON BOROUGHS DISABILITY RESOURCE TEAM: DISABILITY EQUALITY TRAINING

The team's main goal is: 'To challenge some of the common myths and false distinctions that relegate people with disabilities to the status of a discriminated minority.' The team undertake disability training in relation to attitudes towards people with a range of disabilities. All of the disability equality trainers have a disability. Many of the aims of the disability equality training, although broad, could be applied specifically to changing attitudes towards people with learning difficulties.

The training aims:

- To enable participants to 'recognise the discriminatory language and social images that help to perpetuate the inequality of people with disabilities'.

- To change discriminatory beliefs, attitudes and practices.

- To present a social model of disability rather than a medical model, and to highlight the political issues.

- To enable participants to put equal opportunities policy into practical action.

An important point is that 'courses have

been shown to be most useful when the content relates directly to the jobs the people do'. The team have devised tailor made courses for people working in personnel departments, libraries, social services departments and other organisations and institutions. Could similar models be developed to change attitudes towards people with learning difficulties? Could inputs be given to trainee journalists, advertisers and other opinion formers?

Resources

Disability Equality Training — Changing Discriminatory Attitudes and Practices towards People with Disabilities.

Local Authorities Anti-Discriminatory Code of Practice.
    Available from: London Boroughs Disability Resource Team, Bedford House, 125—133 Camden High Street, London NW1. Tel: 071 482 5299

Think for yourself

How did you get your first impressions of a person with a learning difficulty? Have your attitudes changed since that initial encounter?
What have you observed in terms of public images of people with learning difficulties as presented in newspapers, films, books, television, radio and charity advertisements?
If you thought a media image of people with learning difficulties was

biased, what steps could you take to make your views known?
How do you respond if a member of the public makes a negative comment when you are out with one or more students?
How do you react when strangers, colleagues or friends tell you that 'you must be so wonderful to work with these people?'

The following sections describe a range of current initiatives which are positively shaping attitudes towards people with learning difficulties:

- Breaking barriers through drama. The Strathcona Theatre Company works in schools and medical schools to demonstrate their skills and to change attitudes. All of the actors and actresses have learning difficulties.

- Short courses designed to change attitudes. Bolton College and Avon social services have developed short courses to increase people's understanding and awareness of issues relating to people with learning difficulties. An American profile is reproduced which provides a useful starting point for planning courses.

- Public awareness through community involvement. Contact with people in the community has developed positive images for students at the Causeway Centre, whose art was publicly exhibited.

- The integration of Samantha Hulley at Heathcote School, Stevenage, has

caused her school friends and their parents as well as her teachers to reconsider their attitudes towards people with disabilities. Although this example is school-based, it is included to demonstrate how positive attitudes can be fostered in young people through the experience of integration.

BREAKING BARRIERS THROUGH DRAMA: THE STRATHCONA THEATRE COMPANY

Background

'We're professionals. We go on tour everywhere.' (Paul Wakelin.)

The Strathcona Theatre Company is a professional group consisting of 10 actors and actresses, all of whom have learning difficulties, and two directors, Janet Bliss and Joan Greening. The group met at Strathcona Social Education Centre in 1982, and became an independent company in June 1986. It is also a registered charity. From the start the cast have devised their own plays and in the initial stages had to persuade Janet and Joan to act in a support role, as the two directors themselves felt they lacked the necessary skills. It has been a learning process for the entire company, as the directors became adept at organising sound effects and sets and creating developmental drama games, while the cast have developed their skills in drama, dance and mime. They continue to write and perform a new play each year and have worked all over the country giving performances and workshops for a wide variety of audiences.

The members of the cast realise that being in the theatre company has enabled them to develop their skills in a variety of ways:

'I've learnt to speak more slowly and clearly, and how to help people if they get stuck on their lines. I use a tape recorder to learn all my lines because I can't read and write.' (Kenny Vesterfelt)

'I've learnt all sorts of things, like learning directions.' (Spencer Wiafe Ababio)

'We do drama and dance and different games. We think of different ideas and who we want to be. We try acting it out. Some are good at being funny — some are good at dancing — and some are good at speaking.' (Tim Williams)

'I've learnt some French at school and it's helped in the new play where I play a Frenchman. I've learnt how to run workshop sessions.' (John Byrne)

'I've learnt to show people how to do acting. I teach people about drama — show them how the company can act and dance. We try to get them involved in working with the theatre company'. (Pius Hickey)

'Before, I couldn't act at all. Now I do a lot of dancing and acting. I like it a lot.' (Michelle Minner)

Raising Community Awareness in Primary Schools

The company takes its plays and workshops into a variety of settings. One important aspect of the programme is to work with schools and medical schools to break down barriers about people with disabilities. In 1989, the company received a grant from Thames Telethon to take their plays and workshops into primary schools. This initiative has been greatly valued by school staff and children alike.

The pupils are able to enjoy the performance, and then work in groups of about 15 with company members in carefully structured workshops. The pupils have a chance to try some drama and mime for themselves, which is very enjoyable. They work in partnership with company members, sharing and developing ideas. The mutual trust and respect which grows during the contact time reinforces positive images of people with learning difficulties.

A follow-up discussion is held in which the children are asked to talk freely and honestly about their responses to the company, and to ask them questions. Many admit to feeling worried, nervous or scared before the contact with the group:

'Some people say that handicapped people can turn on you.'

'Some people are afraid to touch them.'

The general comments after the workshops indicate that the children's attitudes have been shaped by the positive experience of working with the Strathcona Theatre Company:

'It gets us more used to handicapped people.'

'We've made friends with handicapped people.'

The children are also able to satisfy their curiosity during this session by asking questions such as: 'People with Down's syndrome — do they all look the same?' The actors and actresses help to answer their queries, and clearly value these sessions:

'I think it's a very good idea to work with children. I've never done it before. I like to hear their chat and see what they feel about the theatre company.' (Pius Hickey)

To date, the schools worked with have been in the same area of London as that in which the company members also live. The sense of community is reinforced by the fact that company members are able to say that they live nearby — and they may well meet the children again in the street or at the bus stop.

Strathcona Challenges the 'Medical Model' of Disability

The Strathcona Theatre Company has worked with medical students at St George's Hospital, Tooting, and at St Mary's Hospital, Paddington.

Dr Sheila Hollins, a consultant psychiatrist, works at St George's Medical School in Tooting. She books the Strathcona Theatre Company every three months for a drama performance and workshop for fourth year medical students. For some students it is their first contact with people who have learning difficulties. On the course programme it is deliberately not advertised that the actors and actresses are disabled, so that the medical students arrive without preconceived ideas. The session format is as follows:

1. Performance by Strathcona Theatre Company.

2. Workshop involving medical students working alongside the cast to devise a short play or mime.

3. Question and answer session with the company, in which the medical students ask questions such as 'How do you learn your lines?'

4. After the company has gone, the medical students meet their clinical teachers to discuss the connections between medical concerns and the people they have met.

Dr Hollins observes that the sessions communicate to the prospective doctors that people with learning difficulties are people first. She wants the students to see the person behind the disability and to understand that people with learning difficulties deserve the same quality of health care as other people. Some of the exercises without speech make the medical students more aware of non-verbal communication.

Dr Hollins expects that as a result the students will be alert to the possibilities that people with learning difficulties may need extra help and time to explain what is medically wrong with them, and to understand the treatment that they are offered.

The response of a doctor to an

individual determines the quality of care and treatment that will be given. The medical students are asked to examine their own attitudes and responses to disability.

The comments from medical students after a Strathcona Theatre Company workshop indicate that the experience has had an impact on their perceptions of people with disabilities:

'I feel more relaxed now about meeting people with disabilities.'
'It wasn't as awkward as I'd expected.'
'It was fun!'
'In paediatrics we were told that although small children with Down's Syndrome are friendly, they get difficult when they grow up. But these people were nice and friendly.'

Strengths of Strathcona's Work

- Education of the wider community takes place with Strathcona Company members working on equal terms with various sections of the public.

- Publicity is professionally designed and printed.

Where Next?

The long-term future of the company will soon be a matter for consideration. At present, all company members are part-time. The work is subsidised by grants and fees for performances, but applying for grants takes much time and energy. The directors cope with administration, transport, book balancing and numerous other day-to-day matters, such as keeping the diaries of the 10 cast members up to date. This is in addition to the stress of being on tour, and of constantly dreaming up new ideas for workshops.

Think for yourself

What support structures could be created to sustain educational initiatives such as the creative work developed by the Strathcona Theatre Company?
How could a project like this be started in your area?
How can similar educational initiatives, in which people with and without learning difficulties relate as equals, be developed to promote positive attitudes in a range of settings?

SHORT COURSES DESIGNED TO CHANGE ATTITUDES

Bolton Metropolitan College runs a course entitled 'Know Your Neighbour'. It aims to inform the general public about care in the community in relation to people with learning difficulties or mental health problems. The course is targeted at people living in the areas where hospital residents are being resettled. Publicity is distributed widely in the local area, and an advertisement is put in the local paper to attract prospective students.

Format

The course runs for 10 weeks with each session lasting one-and-a-half hours. It is run in the evening or daytime according to demand. It is double-staffed by tutors with expertise in mental health and learning difficulties.

Students complete a questionnaire when they start the course to document their attitudes in the first week. The course then uses video and discussion to explore issues related to normalisation, community care, learning difficulties and mental health. People with learning difficulties or mental health problems are invited to contribute as paid guest speakers during one session.

In the last week, students again complete a questionnaire about their reactions to people with learning difficulties or mental health problems. A positive shift in attitude can be clearly demonstrated by a comparison of the two questionnaires.

Progression

One measure of the success of the 'Know Your Neighbour' course is to look at the various routes of progression and development that students follow:

- two students have progressed to do a specialist teaching certificate

- one student decided to do a nursing qualification in order to work with people who have learning difficulties

- several people have encouraged their neighbours to attend the course

- some people have been motivated to go on and become volunteers

- one woman used what she had gained from the course to persuade her

husband and son to join her in offering a family placement to an adult with a learning difficulty

- one father was encouraged by a discussion about high expectations promoting development. He went home and successfully taught his son how to use a knife for the first time

- another parent participated in the course and consequently decided that her daughter should have the opportunity to go to a mainstream school.

Think for yourself

Could a 'Know Your Neighbour' style course be piloted in your area? Who would need to be involved? How would it be advertised? How would it be evaluated? How can people with learning difficulties be involved in an active rather than a token way?

'CITIZEN TO CITIZEN': DISABILITY EDUCATION IN AVON

Phil Madden (service manager, Avon social services) is firmly committed to the principle of educating people in the community about issues relating to people with learning difficulties.

A two-day course was offered for two years, run by the extra-mural department of the University of Bristol, under the title 'Citizen to Citizen'. It was tutored by

Phil Madden and a social services colleague. The course was widely advertised, and 20 people enrolled each time. Of these, half worked for agencies such as the police, housing associations and the Department of Social Security. The other half were social workers and community nurses in general roles who had an interest in developing their knowledge.

The course emphasised the difference in the quality of life between living in a hospital and living in the community, using specially-taken slides. Issues of privacy and dignity were raised and discussed. Participants were encouraged to reflect on the main issues in relation to their own roles and jobs, and to think about their personal reaction in responding sensitively to a person with a learning difficulty, whether in a work setting or as a new neighbour.

A visit to an establishment to talk to staff working with people with learning difficulties was arranged for individuals or pairs. Members of a student council were paid as tutors to come and talk to the group. This session was awkward and stilted, and Phil would prefer in future to have an activity session involving students and people with learning difficulties on equal terms.

Course Feed-back from Students

'*It made me think.*'

'*Interesting and helpful.*'

'*It gave me more awareness of problems, issues, possibilities.*'

Since the re-organisation of Avon social services, it has not been possible to repeat the course. It is, however, on the agenda for future action. Phil has been researching parent action and attitude change in America, and hopes to develop some of these ideas.

Think for yourself

Could a course such as 'Getting to Know You' be run in association with a local college, university or polytechnic?
Who would be the target audience?
How would the course be structured?
How would people with learning difficulties be involved in the planning and presentation?

A PROFILE TO PLAN COURSES

Values Into Action (formerly the Campaign for People with Mental Handicaps) organised three conferences on the theme of 'Changing Attitudes' in autumn 1989. Practitioners from New Jersey shared their experiences with a British audience. They use techniques which include puppets for children, drama, role-play, humour, discussion, video and experiential learning. They prepared the Community Education Profile on page 156 and recommend the following steps in developing a programme:

1. *Put a team together*
   Involve for example parents, social services, government agencies and self advocates.

2. *Prioritise needs according to a local level.*
   Target the group that is most affecting the lives of people with disabilities or causing difficulties for service users.
3. *Decide on the message you want to convey and how to present it.*

Further information about the New Jersey approach is available from: Krystal Odell, New Jersey Department of Human Services, Division of Developmental Disabilities, Office of Community Education, CN 700 Trenton, New Jersey 08625, USA.

What would be the most appropriate way to get our message across to this group?

What do I still need to make this presentation feasible?

(New Jersey Department of Human Services, Division of Developmental Disabilities, Office of Community Education.)

COMMUNITY EDUCATION PROFILE

One of the most pressing needs for people with disabilities in my community is ...

What the average person needs to know about disabilities is ...

The place in my community which needs most education about disabilities is ...

What I know about this potential audience is that they are ...

What disability information is available in the community and who is it provided by?

What resources do I have to present to this potential audience?

Who could I work with in my area to provide this presentation?

PUBLIC AWARENESS THROUGH COMMUNITY INVOLVEMENT

At the Causeway Centre in Kingston-upon-Thames, the young and committed staff group all have qualifications in teaching and/or fine art. Students attending this social services day centre can choose from a wide variety of creative activities, including pottery, silk screen printing and stained glass. Students have a choice of activity and are self motivated. They are trusted and given responsibility. For example, in the woodwork room tools are left out rather than locked away. The facilities are excellent and students from the local college come to use the work-rooms. Two of the centre students have progressed to join a GCSE art group at this college. In February 1989 the Causeway Centre mounted an art exhibition at a local church in a busy market place. The advertising poster did not label the artists as having learning difficulties. Members of the general public came in and viewed the artwork, looking at the exhibits and valuing them in their own right rather than because the artists had learning difficulties. One staff member described how this approach stopped the 'sympathy' reaction, and led to the artists and their work being given a positive value. Much care and preparation went into framing, mounting and lighting the display, which was extremely professional. People were on hand to answer queries from the public, who generally commented on the high quality of the work before asking 'What is the Causeway Centre?'

Points to Note

- The art exhibition gave students a focus for their work in a community-based setting.

- The general public were given positive images of the artists. The central location of the church encouraged people to drop in.

- A professional approach was taken in mounting the art exhibition, with an effective publicity poster and a high standard of presentation.

- There is an active link and two-way exchange with the local college, with opportunities for progression and integration.

Think for yourself

How can positive public recognition of the work of the students with learning difficulties be achieved in your local area?

What role can exhibitions, displays and publications play?
How can work be presented to be valued in its own right rather than to attract the 'sympathy vote'?

CHANGING ATTITUDES THROUGH INTEGRATION

Samantha Hulley attends Heathcote School in Stevenage. It is large, bustling comprehensive school. Sam wears school uniform, responds when her name is called on the register and participates fully in the life of the school, just like the rest of the children. Sam has severe learning difficulties, cannot speak and uses a wheelchair.

Sam has made many developments in her skills while at Heathcote School and has also gained socially.

The benefits of Sam's participation at Heathcote School are two-way. As her textiles teacher commented: 'It's been good for her and good for the group.' Sam has had the chance to join in with all of the varied curriculum areas open to her classmates. She will be doing options in the fourth year, like the rest of her class. She has many friends at the school, who spend time with her both at school and in social situations outside school. Sam is regularly invited for parties and meals out with her friends and their families. The children at the school come from the same neighbourhood and local community as Sam, which would not be the case were she still at a special school for children with severe learning difficulties.

The comments from Sam's classmates

demonstrate how her presence has shaped their attitudes in a positive way:

'It's completely changed all of our attitudes towards disabled people. We all know her signs and different noises. She enjoys being with her friends and coming to the school disco. We all stick up for Sam.'

'It's nice to be able to communicate with Sam and to show people you can. Everyone accepts her. It would be silly for her to be in a school for the disabled with people her own level. Here she's been able to pick up some French.'

'Handicapped people are not going to progress much in schools of their own. Here Sam can learn to mix in with all of us. We're helping her and she's helping us. She's treated just like one of us. If she's noisy she's asked to leave the room.'

'It makes you quite aware having Sam in the class, you know — like knowing what to do if someone has a fit.'

Gil Parsons, until recently Sam's support teacher, comments that the children's ready acceptance of Sam has positively influenced the attitudes of teachers and parents. People who were worried about Sam being in the classroom or mixing with their children have changed their views. Sally Morrison, a teacher who has worked with Sam for three years, has also noticed the immense impact that Sam's presence has had on staff and pupils alike. She recalls that at first some staff were outraged at the thought of Sam eating alongside everyone else. Now it is taken for granted that she joins in with the rush of the dinner queue, and gets assistance with eating her choice of meal.

Sam's presence at Heathcote School has enabled the staff and pupils to develop positive images of disability.

Suggested Follow Up

Read *Samantha Goes to School* (Values Into Action Publications, formerly CMH).

See the Open University video *Sam's Story* (1989), which shows Sam fully integrated at Heathcote School.

Read 'Tomorrow will be my dancing day', interpreted from Sam's sounds and signs in *Know Me As I Am* (Hodder and Stoughton, 1990)

Think for yourself

From your experience, how are attitudes formed and changed?
How can the attitudes of the next generation of adults be positively shaped towards people with learning difficulties?
How can wider opportunities for integration be developed, and how will the likely attitude change be reflected?

SUMMARY

Attitudes towards people with learning difficulties can be positively shaped by shared experiences in which people with and without learning difficulties relate on equal terms.

Education of the wider community by means of short courses can be successful. People with learning difficulties themselves should be actively involved in the process.

The influence of media and advertising images on public perceptions of people with learning difficulties requires further investigation and analysis.

FURTHER READING AND RESOURCES

Readings on Public Images of People with Disabilities

Alison Wertheimer *According to the Papers: Press reporting on people with learning difficulties.* Values Into Action, 1988

Susan Scott Parker *They Aren't In The Brief. Advertising people with disabilities.* King's Fund Centre, 1989.

Ann Shearer *Think Positive! Advice on presenting people with mental handicaps.* International League of Societies for Persons with Mental Handicap, 1984. (From: ILSMH, Avenue Louise 248, bte 17, B-1050 Brussels, Belgium.)

Readings on Public Education

Roy McConkey & Bob McCormack *Breaking Barriers. Educating people about disability.* Souvenir Press, 1983.

Roy McConkey *Who Cares?* Souvenir Press, 1987.

David Sines (ed.) *Towards Integration: Comprehensive services for people with mental handicaps.* Harper & Row, 1988.

Phil Madden & Ian Maund 'Getting to know you.' *Community Care*, 16 April 1987.

Staff working for National Children's Homes in Wales have been investigating disability awareness education for children in junior schools in relation to people with learning difficulties. A preliminary report is available, and it is hoped to prepare a teaching package. Details from: Joan Williams, NCH In Wales, St David's Court, 68A Cowbridge Road East, Cardiff CF1 9DN.

Information Leaflets

Meeting People with Mental Handicaps. Values Into Action, Oxford House, Derbyshire Street, London E2 6HG. Tel: 071 729 5436.

Myths about People with Learning Difficulties. Values Into Action (address as above).

Understanding Mental Handicap. MIND Publications, 22 Harley Street, London W1N 2ED. Tel: 071 637 0741.

Information sheets and leaflets on a variety of topics are available from: MENCAP National Centre, 123 Golden Lane, London EC1Y 0RT. Tel: 071 253 9433.

Leaflets on epilepsy are available from: National Information Society, British

Epilepsy Association, 40 Hanover Square, Leeds L53 1BE. Tel: 0345 089599.

Talking about People with Disabilities

It's About Disability: Campaign for real people. National Union of Journalists, Acorn House, 314—320 Gray's Inn Road, London WC1X 8DP. Tel: 071 278 7916.

Information for Journalists. Down's Syndrome Association, 153–155 Mitcham Road, Tooting, London SW17 9PG. Tel: 081 682 4001.

Our Way with Words. The Spastics Society, 12 Park Crescent, London W1N 4EQ. Tel: 071 636 5020.

Videos

If You Let Me video and campaign pack. Barnardos, Tanners Lane, Barkingside, Ilford, Essex IG6 1QG.

Let's Get It Straight. An introduction to people with learning difficulties which can be hired free from MENCAP (address above).

I'm A Loud Mouth. Twentieth Century Vixen, 82A Lordship Lane, London N16 0QP. Tel: 081 802 3911.

The Open University course P555(M) 'Working Together' video shows groups of people with learning difficulties achieving in the creative arts, such as the group 'Heart & Soul' performing at Covent Garden.

Addresses

Strathcona Theatre Company, c/o Janet Bliss/Joan Greening, 1 Heathfield Park, Willesden Green, London NW2 5JE.

Skills for People, Haldane House, Tankerville Terrace, Jesmond, Newcastle-upon-Tyne NE2 3AM. Tel: 091 281 8737. The Speakers' Bureau from this self advocacy project responds to invitations to talk (about disability/labelling) and will travel nationally if expenses are met.

10. Issues for managers and planners

Services are changing and developing in the light of new demands — from the White Paper *Caring for People* to the Education Reform Act. Complex issues are thrown up for managers and planners across agencies. Decisions have to be taken about priorities, costings and effectiveness.

The issues discussed in this chapter were highlighted many times throughout the course of the NIACE Rowntree Project. Transport in particular was mentioned as a barrier to access on virtually all of the field visits made. Low morale amongst staff, who felt isolated and unsupported, was a worrying and common feature of many visits.

There are no ready-made solutions to the questions raised in this section; indeed, it would over-simplify the problems to offer universal answers. A few instances are illustrated where people have started to tackle the difficulties which face many managers, practitioners and students. The organistion of this chapter is as follows.

1: The Principles

- Setting a value base: developing policy.
- Monitoring and evaluating the quality of provision.
- Labels, images and groupings.

2: Barriers to Access

- Transport.
- Buildings.

- Fees.
- Curriculum.
- Attitudes.

3: Equal Opportunities?

- Age, race, gender and learning difficulties.

4: Steps Forward

- Resourcing provision.
- Staff development and support.
- A multi-agency framework.

5: Towards New Ways of Organising Learning

- Recommendations for managers and planners to consider with practitioners.

6: Framework for Development: A self-questionnaire

- The results of this profile can be used as a basis for review, development and change.

1: THE PRINCIPLES

Setting a Value Base: Developing Policy

Developing a shared philosophy and a common vision is recognised as the foundation for building effective change and progress in services, from management to grassroots level.

Monitoring and Evaluating the Quality of Provision

Criteria must be set for monitoring and evaluating the quality of provision. Some providers have opted for quantity rather than quality of provision for adults with learning difficulties, with disastrous results.

Quality is an issue for managers and staff. High quality provision is based on sound ideals and philosophy translated into practice by well-trained and supported staff. A number of managers think that 'special needs' staff do 'a great job' and steer well away from the territory, without examining the quality of work taking place. Decisions need to be taken about who will evaluate, how and when. The checklist on pages 178 to 181 will help managers and practitioners to identify the strengths and needs of provision.

Managers need to consider outcomes and performance indicators in order to justify expenditure. Ways in which learning services can be monitored must be considered. Approaches can include:

- Asking tutors to outline plans in advance and then to account for what has actually happened. Positive outcomes might be: maintenance of skills; development of skills; growth in confidence, alertness, awareness, self-esteem or self advocacy.

- Direct feedback can be obtained from students, parents/carers as keyworkers, as well as from tutors.

- Tutors can swap roles to observe each other's classes in order to give support and to offer constructive criticism.

- Advice and support can be obtained from the relevant inspection/advisory service.

Although certification is an option for some students with learning difficulties, for many the growth of self-esteem and confidence gained from education will be justification in itself for maintaining expenditure on provision. For others, tutors will be able to comment on the development of skills. What can a student do or achieve now that he or she was unable to do before?

Managers should be prepared to change their perceptions in the light of evaluations. 'Group X' may not have developed practical skills as fast as the tutor anticipated — but the group processes, ability to listen and to negotiate combined with the effects of a growth in self worth can present valid reasons to continue funding. In *Performance Indicators and the Education of Adults* (UDACE, 1989), the point is made that for adults, learning outcomes may include 'unforeseen or accidental' benefits, which are described as 'windfall gains.' Social and personal development is seen as a valid outcome of learning: 'The education and training of adults should be measured in terms relevant to the purposes of the service, including such factors as personal development, learner autonomy and equity' (*ibid.*).

Think for yourself

How is monitoring and evaluation of the learning service currently implemented?
What improvements could be made? How?
How can the views of staff, students and relatives be considered when reviewing provision?

Some tutors of adults with learning difficulties are expected to teach a wide range of subjects — for example, art, cookery, literacy, gardening, etc. However, tutors with a specialist background in particular subjects will bring knowledge, skills and depth to their work that generalists cannot easily reproduce. This has implications for the quality of work, and for staff development/support. Co-tutoring provides one model.

From Beans on Toast to Cordon Bleu. In Luton, Helen Fletcher, from Special Adult Learning Programmes, has teamed up with Kathy Holmes, a specialist cookery lecturer at Barnfield College, to offer provision for students with severe learning difficulties from a nearby day centre. The sharing of skills and enthusiasm has been beneficial to tutors and students alike. Helen has been able to help Kathy negotiate the programme with students, and to break skills down into small steps. Kathy has moved Helen away from basic survival cookery and successfully taught students to use sharp implements and to learn new techniques, based on recipes students have chosen. Helen has been amazed as students have exceeded her initial expectations. Kathy's specialist expertise has been an important factor in the successful co-tutoring. As one student said 'I feel like a proper chef now.'

Labels, Images and Groupings

Public images present powerful messages. How students with learning difficulties are described — where and how they learn and what they learn — these factors determine how other people will view them and will also have an impact on the self-image of the students. One college section has avoided the label 'special needs' by describing provision as 'extended education', which is less stigmatising for students with learning difficulties.

2: BARRIERS TO ACCESS

Transport

'I got here on my own this morning on the bus, for the first time. I got a number 9 and then a 12. I thought to myself — I feel like doing it. Now I've proved to myself that I can do it! I feel great.'
(Adult education student.)

The majority of students with learning difficulties cannot participate in learning activities at adult and further education establishments unless transport is provided or unless transport training is facilitated. Transport to and from educational groups and activities presented a major challenge to all of the providers visited during the course of the project.

An investment in time and money is necessary to enable people who do not yet have the skills to travel independently to take part in provision. The following approaches have all been employed by practitioners:

- investing staff time in developing transport training

- teaching a student to make a journey independently in the most appropriate way

- a more able student can help a less confident student to make a journey

- volunteer drivers — either for private cars or a minibus. Petrol costs and insurance need to be considered

- local Dial-A-Ride schemes, in which a door-to-door service plus escort is provided

- taxis

- other agencies (health or social services, voluntary organisations) are sometimes able to offer transport, as are parents/relatives or support workers

- minibus driven by a member of staff — borrowed for the occasion, shared with a day centre or owned by the provider

- students attending an adult education centre can offer lifts to students with learning difficulties.

Buildings

For the minority of students with learning difficulties who have physical disabilities, access to buildings presents a major barrier. At one college, students with learning difficulties who have physical disabilities can only use ground-floor facilities. This prevents them from learning to cook and from making full use of the college library, as both facilities are upstairs.

The quality and location of accommodation offered to students with learning difficulties is often low status. This situation is unacceptable.

Fees

Tuition costs should not present a barrier to learning for students with learning difficulties. Most areas offer remission of fees for students with disabilities.

In Richmond, an adult education voucher scheme is in operation which benefits people on low incomes, including adults with learning difficulties. For £6, a set of three vouchers can be purchased in order to gain access to three different 'full priced', mainstream adult education classes. In this way, a word processing course, normally costing £35, can be studied for the reduced fee of £2. Two major charities subsidise the scheme, which has opened up integrated opportunities for a large number of

students with learning difficulties, amongst others.

Curriculum

Access to the curriculum is restricted for students with learning difficulties if learning options are narrow (based on literacy, numeracy and life skills) and if they are presented in a written format. (See Chapter 3 for a wider discussion.)

Attitudes

'I don't like these handicapped students cluttering up the corridors' (senior college manager).

Negative attitudes can prevent students with learning difficulties being welcomed and accepted in a learning environment.

Positive steps can be taken to educate people at a variety of levels in colleges as A Special Professionalism sets out (DES, 1987).

At Northumberland College, teaching staff planned and implemented a one-day course for senior managers and college governors to explain their philosophy and approach to working with students with special educational needs. The tutors' view is that special needs work is an issue for the whole establishment, and not just for a couple of key staff. (See Chapter 9 for a wider discussion.)

Think for yourself

How is transport currently organised for students with learning difficulties?
How can improvements be planned,

funded and actioned?
How can travel training for independence be resourced and implemented?
What modifications are necessary to make buildings accessible for people with physical disabilities?
How can alterations be planned, funded and actioned?
Is there a policy on fee remission for students with learning difficulties? If not, could one be developed?
Does this apply to all classes, or only to 'special' classes?
Is the curriculum organised so that students with learning difficulties can make informed choices from the widest possible range of options?
Are learning options presented in formats helpful to students with learning difficulties, i.e. not in the traditional written format?
Do senior staff and managers, teaching staff and ancillary staff have positive attitudes towards students with learning difficulties and their educational rights?
If not, could an awareness-raising exercise be planned and implemented?

3: EQUAL OPPORTUNITIES? AGE, RACE, GENDER AND LEARNING DIFFICULTIES

The position of NIACE as an equal opportunities organisation is that age, race, gender and disability should not present barriers to learning. NIACE believes that equal opportunities policies and practices should reflect these values.

Age

Some education establishments have inflexible, age-based entry criteria for students with learning difficulties. One college offering a range of provision insists that students must be under 30 years of age. This policy has led to the exclusion of older adults who are keen to learn. (It has also led to social services staff inventing new dates of birth for prospective students.)

Age should not exclude students with learning difficulties from educational opportunities. As schools for children with severe learning difficulties were not opened until 1971, the majority of older adults with learning difficulties have received no formal educational opportunities. A minority of places offer 'pre-retirement' courses for older adults with learning difficulties.

At Prudhoe Hospital in Northumberland a group of women aged 85 and 86 are learning to cook for the first time in their lives. They have a wonderful time learning 'down at the bakery', as they describe it.

Race

There is little evidence of multicultural work in learning opportunities for adults with learning difficulties. Students from black and other ethnic minority groups are rarely offered provision that is culturally sensitive to their needs and experiences.

At Newham Community College, a course was run for black women with learning difficulties, tutored by two black women tutors. The course examined the multiple oppressions experienced by the participants in terms of race, gender and disability. Time was given to consider various religions, music, foods and family backgrounds. Different cultures were celebrated, and positive images of black women were presented in pictures and books. The students developed in self-esteem and identity and became more assertive — for instance in requesting a course in dressmaking for Asian women. The course was only funded for a short period. The co-ordinator is currently recommending that the provision should become an integral part of the college provision.

At Streatham and Tooting Adult Education Institute, the needs of students from different ethnic backgrounds are actively responded to. Students with learning difficulties have joined groups in 'Black Studies', and in 'Afro-Caribbean Cookery'. Multicultural days are held where students can try on saris, taste different foods and participate in music and dance from other countries.

In Harrow, English as a Second Language provision is offered to students with learning difficulties who want to improve their English.

These examples were isolated. Other areas need to examine their policy and practice for students with learning difficulties from ethnic minorities. This may involve consultation exercises and the translation of publicity materials into relevant languages. The building of learning options appropriate to the needs of students with learning difficulties from different racial backgrounds needs consideration. For example, learning to make chapattis and curry rather than English food, or learning to go to a temple or mosque rather than a church will be culturally appropriate for some students from India and Pakistan.

Gender

Equality of opportunity for women with learning difficulties has yet to be achieved in some places. The project received details from several establishments where sex stereotyping still prevails and where for instance cookery is still largely seen as a 'female' subject. A number of 'men only' groups participate in gardening or engineering. Other schemes offered more positive images, where, for instance young women with learning difficulties were learning bricklaying.

Severity of Learning Difficulty

In some cases it is the students with the most severe learning difficulties who miss out on education. An additional physical disability, an inability to communicate or 'difficult' behaviour may cause potential students to be excluded. See Chapter 7 for a discussion of the benefits of learning for these students.

Additional staffing is necessary to cater for students with such disabilities. Extra tutors, non-teaching assistants and volunteers have all been used to give the necessary support.

Think for yourself

Is policy for students with special educational needs embedded in a wider framework of policy on equal opportunities?

How can learning opportunities be made available to older adults with learning difficulties?

How can the learning needs of students with learning difficulties from black and other ethnic minority groups be adequately assessed and addressed?

Is the full range of learning options open to both women and men? How can women with learning difficulties be encouraged to try subjects which may be new to them — such as bricklaying or woodwork?

Are students excluded from education if their learning difficulties are too severe?

If so, how could this situation be remedied?

4: STEPS FORWARD

To develop educational opportunities for adults with learning difficulties, policy, evaluation of provision, equal opportunities and barriers to access are all important issues, as outlined above. Three further aspects require consideration:

- resourcing provision

- a multi-agency framework

- staff development and support.

Resourcing Provision

Under the Education Reform Act (1988), local education authorities have a duty to 'secure the provision for their area of adequate facilities for further education.' They are also required to 'have regard to the requirements of persons over compulsory school age who have learning difficulties.'

The Education Reform Act required LEAs' schemes of delegation for further education to be approved by the Secretary of State, to take effect from 1 April 1990. The majority of freestanding adult education services are outside of and unaffected by the legislation, unless the LEA has specifically written them into ERA planning. LEAs have, however, been required to use funding formulae to work out budgets and to distribute additional costs of certain provision. Special educational needs can be designated as a programme area (Circular 9/88), which can be given an advantageous programme weight. Colleges providing for students with special educational needs can thus be given a favourable and local programme weight in order to offset additional costs, for example a higher staff/student ratio or specialist equipment.

The schemes of delegation are fixed as from April 1990. Major modifications (such as proposing a new college or programme area) require a resubmission to the Secretary of State. Minor modifications (adjusting weightings or altering the equation of how many part-time hours add up to one full-time student, for example) can take place at a local level. However, the 'cake' of resources remains the same overall size —

the 'slices' can be made a different size.

ERA requires colleges to develop further education provision from delegated budgets. In addition, the local education authority development fund can be used to develop provision in colleges for adults with learning difficulties because 'the development of provision for those with special educational needs may need pump priming and funding for projects' (Circular 9/88).

Think for yourself

Has a budget been devised which will advantageously resource students with learning difficulties at the local college(s) of further education? Strategic plans will be revised annually under ERA. How can provision for adults with learning difficulties be promoted at this stage, using the monitoring/review procedures recommended by UDACE? (See Securing Adequate Facilities. *UDACE, 1988.)*

What opportunities for setting up new projects or pump priming could be funded from the LEA's development fund?

How can the provision developed at freestanding adult education centres (which are not covered by schemes of delegation) be protected and expanded?

DES Circular 8/88 outlines the composition of an FE college governing body. It is possible to co-opt a specialist in special educational needs. Has this step been taken?

Good Provision — What Price?

Local Education Authorities have a choice about whether to include independent adult education as a programme area in formulating funding for further education. This aspect of planning has implications for the full range of post school education provision. Is it possible to fix an appropriate level or resource weighting across the post school sector? Is it possible to determine the cost of good provision?

Needs Analysis

Needs must be identified clearly in order to rationalise funding. Writing a policy and rationale will help to ensure the best application of funds to develop learning opportunities for adults with learning difficulties.

In a time of diminishing resources, it is important to think creatively about possible sources of funding. Various schemes and initiatives have been funded by:

- LEAs

- social services departments

- health authorities

- voluntary organisations

- joint finance (See *Care and Education in the Community* by Peter Lavender, FEU, 1989, for a full explanation)

- European Social Fund

- REPLAN (for work with unemployed adults)

- Urban Aid programme

- Training Agency (Youth Training Scheme, Employment Training, Work-Related FE Development Fund)

- charitable donations/trusts

- commercial sponsorship

- ALBSU

- fees paid by parents/individuals/ LEAs.

In view of the dearth of educational work with adults with learning difficulties from black and other ethnic communities, Section XI Home Office funding may be an appropriate source of funds to develop this area of work.

Think for yourself

How many prospective students are there, and what strategies will be used to identify them and to quantify and meet their learning needs? Is the area of work defensible and expandable in the eyes of senior managers and officers?
How can service delivery be ensured?
What statutory legislation can be used to develop provision?
What is the existing budget?
What new initiatives can be justified and funded?
Should there be a financial entitlement for each adult with learning difficulties which guarantees access to learning?

A Multi-agency Framework

Some educational provision for adults with learning difficulties is arranged in relative isolation from contact and involvement with professionals from other agencies. Working closely together across agencies offers significant benefits and is an effective way of:

- Maximising resources by co-working.

Example: Health and education staff in Lancashire jointly run computer aided learning centres in two long stay hospitals.

- Saving duplication by offering a rational and coherent range of learning options across agencies.

Example: At Lisson Grove Social Education Centre, staff from social services and adult education work together to provide the widest possible range of learning options.

- Working towards goals across services.

Example: In Bedfordshire a strategic plan has been developed and implemented by staff from health, social services, education and voluntary organisations.

- Learning from the experiences of other agencies.

Example: In Brighton a staff development day on the education of adults with learning difficulties was held. Health and social services staff offered inputs to education tutors, who reciprocated. Topics included assertiveness, epilepsy and teaching strategies.

- Developing responsiveness to emerging needs.

Example: Attendance at inter-agency meetings highlights areas and developments to which education can contribute.

Staff Support and Development

A feeling of low morale was commonly reported on project visits which is a matter for serious concern. Education tutors working with adults with learning difficulties often teach in challenging and isolated situations, from locked wards on long-stay hospitals to peripatetic teaching at a succession of social services day centres and hostels.

Difficulties Experienced by Staff

'Perennial frustrations! Stress. Every single thing is a fight.'
    'Waiting six years for an order to arrive.'
        'Staff burn out, stress and sickness.'
        'We're not in the business of being profitable ... other areas in the college will always have priority.'
        'Being expected by my boss to fiddle my register to make my group seem larger than it actually is.'

Many staff reported feeling unsupported by their immediate managers, who 'left them to get on with it'. A number of practitioners visited who were involved in high quality work left their jobs during the course of the project, often due to frustration and the feeling that their work was not being adequately recognised or supported.

A clear sense emerged that tutors felt that their work was not being valued.

'Of course, it's much harder to teach A-levels, you know' (comment to tutor of adults with learning difficulties).

Often the students with learning difficulties themselves were not valued by other members of staff, which reinforced the sense of low worth:

'I'm not having those students in the same lift as my students' (head of college department to tutor working with adults with learning difficulties).

Work with adults with learning difficulties is seen as being low status. It is graded at the lowest Burnham grading (Grade V) for part-time work (see *Burnham: The Biggest Barrier of All?* National Bureau for Students with Disabilities, 1986) and career progression is limited. A sense of struggle and frustration came across clearly. Tutors constantly have to defend and justify their work to sceptics, while also having to battle with negative attitudes towards their students. The tension is highlighted by the perceived lack of support from a number of managers.

What can be done?

- Opportunities for regular individual support meetings for all staff should be made available.

Example: At Lisson Grove Social Education Centre in Paddington, all staff have a weekly individual support meeting with a senior colleague.

- Regional and national networking can provide a series of useful contacts for mutual support.

Example: The Adult Literacy and Basic Skills Unit funded a staff development group called 'Adult Basic Education in the Community for People with Severe Learning Difficulties'. Representatives from counties in East Anglia were able to meet and discuss issues of concern. Visits and speakers were also arranged. All participants found the sessions invaluable. Contacts were made, ideas were shared and informal mutual support was offered.

Example: The data gathered for the NIACE Rowntree project has resulted in formal and informal contacts and links being made between authorities and between practitioners.

Example: The South of England has a network for tutors working with students who have learning difficulties, which circulates copies of worksheets which people have developed.

Example: Skill, the National Bureau for Students with Disabilities, has a network of regional groups.

- LEAs and trade unions need to review the status of reimbursement with regard to the element in funding formulae for FE colleges.

Staff Development

Staff development is a key issue in the education of adults with learning difficulties, which affects workers across agencies.

Residential Work. '
a 'carer' to being a.
change of approach.

Social Services Day Centres. A recent inspection report from the Social Services Inspectorate (*Individuals, Programmes and Plans*) comments that a number of day centre staff have received no information about teaching techniques or how people learn.

Health Authority Staff. Nursing staff and occupational therapists are actively involved in teaching people with learning difficulties new skills both in hospital and in community settings.

Adult and Further Education Staff. A large number of staff are part-time and can be 'hard to reach' unless they are paid to attend training, which is rare. Organising a time and a place to suit part-timers (who may have many other commitments, including teaching elsewhere) is complex. Full-time staff can benefit from in service training, which should reach generalists as well as specialists.

Think for yourself

There are several questions that need to be considered in planning training and staff development:
What will the objectives be?
Which staff are being targeted?
What development is needed?
Who will carry out the training?
What methods will be used?

> *What existing staff development materials or packages can be used or adapted?*

Local Initiatives

Some areas have developed their own courses in relation to perceived needs.

- In Avon LEA, a certificate course has been developed for tutors working with adults who have special educational needs. In addition, staff build up a portfolio of additional courses which they have attended.

- Courses in working with adults who have multiple and complex learning difficulties have been developed by the WEA (Western District) and by Orchard Hill FE Centre, Carshalton (Chapter 7).

- Joint initiatives involving multi-agency staff development and training have been set up. Barriers are broken down as staff share experiences, learn together and start to understand each other's approach and jargon. Examples include: A BSc degree in Care and Education in the Community in *Norwich* is being studied by staff across agencies. In *Bedfordshire*, joint finance has established a multi-agency training unit. Courses are open to staff from health, social services, education and voluntary organisations. National trainers visit to offer staff development at the unit's base. In *Brighton*, several multi-agency days

have been mounted by a social services co-ordinator who develops learning opportunities for adults with learning difficulties in local colleges.

National Resources and Courses

This section does not set out to be a comprehensive guide to what is on offer or where, but looks briefly at some recent initiatives.

- Essex adult basic education service in collaboration with Anglia College is offering a part-time RSA Diploma in teaching and learning in adult basic education. It is a generic course, which offers a new specialist option on teaching students with severe learning difficulties.

- Special educational needs post-school is a national priority for money from LEA Training Grants Scheme (LEATGS).

- The special education section at Bristol Polytechnic now has a full-time lecturer working on staff development for tutors of adults with learning difficulties.

- A two-year full-time certificate in the further education and training of adults with learning difficulties is offered at four centres.

- Special educational needs is the focus of some initial full-time training courses for further education staff.

- Diplomas and MEd degrees are developing which concentrate on provision for adults with special educational needs.

- NIACE has mounted two national one-day conferences on the theme of education and community care.

- NIACE REPLAN has organised two national one-day conferences dealing with learning opportunities for unemployed adults with special educational needs.

- The Open University courses 'Patterns for Living' and 'Changing Perspectives' are designed for study by staff working in various settings and agencies. Multi-agency study groups involving parents and users have been highly successful in the former course.

Think for yourself

How are the training needs of staff working in an educational role with adults with learning difficulties:
- *identified?*
- *assessed in terms of priority?*
- *responded to?*

How are training courses developed and evaluated?

What use is made of existing staff development materials?

Could a portfolio system for staff be developed?

How can effective multi-agency training be established?

Who would need to be involved?

How would it be funded and organised?

Resources for Staff Development

Sources of staff development materials relevant to the education of adults with learning difficulties include:

The Further Education Unit, Grove House, 2-6 Orange Street, London WC2H 7WE.

SKILL (National Bureau for Students with Disabilities), 336 Brixton Road, London SW9 7AA.

The Open University, Walton Hall, Milton Keynes MK7 6AA.

Short courses with a national catchment are regularly offered by:

Castle Priory College, Thames Street, Wallingford, Oxfordshire OX10 0HE.

British Institute of Mental Handicap, Wolverhampton Road, Kidderminster, Worcestershire DY10 3PP.

5: TOWARDS NEW WAYS OF ORGANISING LEARNING

Recommendations for managers and planners to consider with practitioners.

1. **The Principles**

   1.1 An analysis of needs should be carried out in each local education authority in liaison with key agencies to ascertain:

   - the potential number of students with learning difficulties

   - the variety and cost of provision which will be required to meet the learning needs identified.

1.2 A policy for the education of adults with learning difficulties should be developed with a linked action plan and resources for implementation.

1.3 Opportunities for learning should be available to all adults with learning difficulties.

1.4 Consideration should be given to a financial entitlement for each adult with learning difficulties to guarantee access to learning.

1.5 The quality of provision should be monitored and evaluated.

1.6 Attention should be given to ensure that labels, images and accommodation associated with a learning service for people with learning difficulties are positive and enhancing rather than stigmatising. Students with learning difficulties should not be accommodated in marginalised or substandard rooms, and should share access to all facilities.

1.7 Educational prospectuses should contain a statement welcoming applications from students with disabilities.

2. Barriers to Access

2.1 Transport requires a substantial investment of resources to ensure that people with learning difficulties are able to participate in adult learning. Investment should be made in developing the skills of students in using public transport.

2.2 Buildings may require adaptations to enable access by people with learning difficulties who have additional physical disabilities or sensory impairment.

2.3 The payment of fees should not present a barrier to learning.

2.4 Learning options should be:

- wide ranging

- presented in a format accessible to students with learning difficulties.

3. Equal Opportunities

3.1 Age, gender, race, social class and severity of learning difficulty should not limit opportunities for learning.

3.2 Policy on special educational needs should be embedded in a wider policy on equal opportunities.

4. Resourcing Provision:Finance and Staffing

4.1 Co-operation and collaboration between agencies is essential to maximise availability and use of resources in terms of staffing, finance and physical resources.

4.2 Ways of funding and joint funding the expansion of educational provision need to be found and guaranteed. Funding formulae under the Education Reform Act should give a favourable weighting to adults with learning difficulties studying at further education colleges.

4.3 Staff support systems should be coherent and should be integral to provision.

4.4 Staff development should be available on a multi-agency basis to share expertise and to break down role barriers between professionals.

4.5 Extra staffing support is necessary to support the learning needs of certain groups and to support certain situations where one to one support is essential. This includes:

- people with challenging behaviour
- people with very severe learning difficulties
- people who are institutionalised
- situations where one to one tuition is necessary: road safety, transport training, teaching job skills in context.

4.6 Where volunteers are used, they should be given initial and continuing support and training. References should be taken up.

4.7 Flexible ways of staffing should be considered: for example a community nurse and an adult education tutor jointly running a group.

4.8 The disparity in conditions of service between different agencies remains a block to progress. Education managers should arrange extended year provision for staff working with adults who have learning difficulties, with extra staff cover or leave taken on a rota.

5. Towards New Ways of Organising Learning

Educational services for adults with learning difficulties need to adapt and change to ensure that the following areas are covered by policy and practice.

5.1 A broad curriculum range should be developed with opportunities for educational guidance and counselling (see Chapters 3 and 5).

5.2 All learning should promote the development of self advocacy. Specific courses should be offered to develop self advocacy skills. Consideration should be given to the role of citizen advocates for students unable to communicate (Chapter 2).

5.3 Opportunities for integration and progression should be developed which provide support, in preference to 'the readiness trap' (Chapter 6).

5.4 The role of learning in community care initiatives should be recognised as a priority and resourced accordingly (Chapter 8).

6. Flexibility

Flexible ways of working are essential in the evolution of new services, which should aim to:

6.1 Offer a wide range of learning options which are sensitive to the preferred learning style of the student (Chapter 4).

6.2 Offer provision on an extended year model. Short courses, drop in facilities and home tuition should be offered alongside more traditional provision. At Bolton College, staff working with adults with learning difficulties take their holidays on a rota throughout the year, rather than on an academic year basis. This enables staff to run summer schools and to keep in contact with students and professionals from other agencies.

6.3 Develop multi-agency links, co-working and staff development.

6.4 Secure funding from a variety of sources.

6: FRAMEWORK FOR DEVELOPMENT

Key areas in the development of continuing education for adults with learning difficulties are set out with questions to reflect on. Tick an appropriate box after considering whether the particular aspect of provision is:

1. non-existent

2. under-developed

3. developed

4. well-developed.

The resulting profile will give a framework for development. It can be used as a basis for review, development and change.

Checklist of Good Practice: A Self-Completion Questionnaire

Needs analysis 1 2 3 4 ☐ ☐ ☐ ☐
Has a mapping exercise taken place to establish likely numbers of potential students?
Have students and relatives/carers been consulted about the sort of educational service they want?
Have other agencies been consulted to draw resources and ideas together?

Policy/philosophy 1 2 3 4 ☐ ☐ ☐ ☐
Is there a written policy on continuing education for adults with learning difficulties?
Is there an action plan with targets set with regard to what is to be achieved, by when and by whom?
Have resources been allocated to implement the action plan?

Aims/objectives 1 2 3 4 ☐ ☐ ☐ ☐
Are the aims and objectives of the learning service clearly defined?

Inter-agency links 1 2 3 4 ☐ ☐ ☐ ☐
Are there formal links between managers and planners of different services?
Is adult, community and further education represented by an appropriate person at joint care planning level?
Are there good working links at a practitioner (grassroots) level?

Delivery of services 1 2 3 4 ☐ ☐ ☐ ☐
Are both full-time and part-time learning

opportunities offered?

Are flexible learning opportunities (short courses, drop in sessions, etc.) offered on an extended year basis?

Breadth of curriculum

1	2	3	4
☐	☐	☐	☐

Is the curriculum wide ranging?
Does it focus narrowly on a 'deficiency' remedial model, or does it offer the full range of learning options open to other students?

Accessibility of curriculum

1	2	3	4
☐	☐	☐	☐

How are learning options chosen?
Have alternatives to the written prospectus been developed?
Are taster sessions available so that students can make informed choices about learning based on direct experience?

Quality of curriculum

1	2	3	4
☐	☐	☐	☐

How is quality monitored and evaluated?
Are subject specialists employed and supported or are special educational needs staff expected to 'have a go' at teaching everything?

Assessment procedures

1	2	3	4
☐	☐	☐	☐

Is assessment a process which actively involves students in developing their own learning targets?
Is assessment done *with* students rather than *to* them?
Is it based on strengths and interests rather than a 'deficiency' model?

Student participation

1	2	3	4
☐	☐	☐	☐

Are students involved in making decisions about what to learn, how and where?
Are students involved in wider planning

processes within the service, for instance in student committees commenting on provision?

Self advocacy

1	2	3	4
☐	☐	☐	☐

Are courses offered in developing self advocacy?
Are courses offered in skills for meetings for self advocates?
Are opportunities for self determination and decision making built into all learning options?

Citizen advocacy

1	2	3	4
☐	☐	☐	☐

Do students unable to speak for themselves have citizen advocates to represent their learning rights and interests?

Learning materials/resources

1	2	3	4
☐	☐	☐	☐

Are learning materials clearly organised and accessible to both tutors and students?
Are learning materials adult and age appropriate?
Do tutors have structured opportunities to find out what is in the resources bank and how to use it?
Is time allocated for the development of new resources?

Opportunities for progression

1	2	3	4
☐	☐	☐	☐

Are opportunities for progression built into learning programmes?
Are options for moving on from provision discussed by tutors and students?
Are 'What Next?' style courses offered which concentrate on progression?

Opportunities for integration **1 2 3 4** ☐ ☐ ☐ ☐
Are opportunities provided for integration into a variety of settings?
Does learning take place in centres used by other adult learners in the community rather than in segregated environments?

Care in the community **1 2 3 4** ☐ ☐ ☐ ☐
Has policy and practice been developed with regard to the role of education in local Care in the Community initiatives?

Community involvement **1 2 3 4** ☐ ☐ ☐ ☐
What involvement is there with people from the local community?
What image do people from the local community have of the learning service?
Do students interact positively and on equal terms with people from the local community —sharing adult education classes, work and leisure facilities?

Community-based learning **1 2 3 4** ☐ ☐ ☐ ☐
Are regular opportunities provided for learning to take place in a community setting rather than in a classroom? (For instance, learning to use community facilities such as libraries, shops and transport.)

Staff development programme **1 2 3 4** ☐ ☐ ☐ ☐
Are in-service courses provided on teaching students with learning difficulties?
Do staff have opportunities to go on national courses and certificated courses?
Is a portfolio system used to record training events attended by tutors?

Staff support system **1 2 3 4** ☐ ☐ ☐ ☐
Are regular individual support meetings offered?
Are there opportunities for staff to share ideas and offer support to each other in a local or regional group?

Level of funding **1 2 3 4** ☐ ☐ ☐ ☐
Is securing ongoing funding for provision viewed as a priority?
Have opportunities for joint finance been explored?
Have students with learning difficulties been given a favourable financial weighting in college of further education budgets?

Physical access **1 2 3 4** ☐ ☐ ☐ ☐
What steps have been taken or need to be taken to enable students with learning difficulties who have additional physical disabilities or sensory impairment to obtain access to educational provision?

Transport **1 2 3 4** ☐ ☐ ☐ ☐
Have resources been invested in transport or transport training to enable students with learning difficulties to travel to and from educational provision?

Advice and guidance **1 2 3 4** ☐ ☐ ☐ ☐
What educational guidance and counselling opportunities are used by students with learning difficulties?
Is there scope for development?

Publicity **1 2 3 4** ☐ ☐ ☐ ☐
Do adult, community and further education prospectuses contain a statement welcoming applications from students with learning

difficulties?

Do publicity materials present positive visual images and descriptions of students with learning difficulties?

	1	2	3	4
Accommodation/environment	□	□	□	□

Is learning situated in main buildings used by other adult learners?

Do students with learning difficulties have access to all departments and facilities in adult and further education establishments?

Do displays of work reflect an adult approach, which values the work of the students?

	1	2	3	4
Gender issues	□	□	□	□

Are women and men given encouragement and opportunities to learn non-traditional subjects?

	1	2	3	4
Race issues	□	□	□	□

Are learning programmes sensitive to the needs of students from black and other ethnic minority groups?

Are consultation programmes being carried out with people from black and other ethnic minority groups, using mother tongue languages if necessary?

	1	2	3	4
Age issues	□	□	□	□

Are older students given opportunities for learning?

	1	2	3	4
Additional complications	□	□	□	□

Are students with learning difficulties who have additional complications (such as challenging behaviour or profound and multiple learning difficulties) included in educational provision?

	1	2	3	4
Cross-agency delivery	□	□	□	□

Are learning programmes being planned in liaison with other agencies?

Are co-tutoring situations encouraged, whereby staff from different agencies team teach?

Is multi-agency staff development taking place?

	1	2	3	4
Relationship with relatives/	□	□	□	□

carers

Are relatives/carers consulted and involved with students and tutors in planning, implementing and reinforcing learning programmes?

Are learning opportunities provided for relatives/carers?

FURTHER READING AND RESOURCES

Handicap, Disability and Special Learning Needs. Guide to good practice in FHE. NATFHE, 1985.

Developing Effective Policy Statements. Guidance notes for college staff who are developing policy statements regarding students with special educational needs. Skill (National Bureau for Students with Disabilities), 1987.

Flexible Learning Opportunities and Special Educational Needs. Further Education Unit, 1988.

The Forgotten Majority. Promoting public transport for people with special needs. Association of Metropolitan Authorities, 1989.

Wolf Wolfensberger & Susan Thomas *Program Analysis of Service Systems' Implementatior of Normalization Goals.* NIRM, 1983.

CMHERA runs courses about the PASS and PASSING systems, which evaluate services in the light of Wolfensberger's work on normalisation or social role valorisation. Accommodation, groupings and use of time are evaluated to see what sort of social images the service conveys. Details from: Paul Williams, CMHERA, 69 Wallingford Road, Oxfordshire RG8 0HL. Tel: 0491 873522.

Burnham: The Biggest Barrier of All? Skill (National Bureau for Students with Disabilities), 1986.

Individuals, Programmes and Plans. Inspection of day services for people with a mental handicap. Social Services Inspectorate at the Department of Health, 1989.

Jan Porterfield *Positive Monitoring. A method of supporting staff and improving services for people with learning disabilities.* BIMH, 1987.

Education Reform Act 1988. Special Needs Briefing. NIACE, 1988.

'Securing Adequate Facilities'. Planning for the education of adults. UDACE, 1988.

Performance Indicators and the Education of Adults. An initial commentary. UDACE, 1989.

Adults and the Act. The Education Reform Act 1988 and adult learners. UDACE, 1988.

Understanding Learning Outcomes. UDACE, 1989.

An Agenda for Access. UDACE, 1990.

Linda Averill, Heather Lee & David Felce *A Guide to Training Resources in Mental Handicap.* BIMH, 1989.

GLOSSARY

Carer: Person with a responsibility in attending to the day-to-day domestic needs of a person with a learning difficulty. For the purpose of this text, a carer may be a parent or sibling, a residential worker or a nurse, for example.

Curriculum: Word which sums up the processes of the learning cycle.

Mainstream: Word commonly used to describe education for people without special educational needs. It is exclusive rather than inclusive, hence the word has not been advocated in the handbook.

Special: Label often used to describe segregated provision set up for students with learning difficulties. Words used in a similar way include discrete and closed.

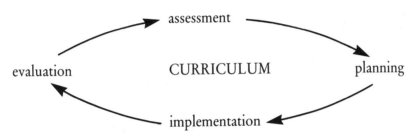

Integration: The process of enabling people with learning difficulties to share places and activities alongside other people. In educational terms for people with learning difficulties this means access to colleges and adult education centres, and access to learning alongside other adults. Classes may also be described as 'integrated', 'open' or 'mainstream'. (See definition of 'mainstream'.)

Learning difficulties: A developmental delay in learning, which may be on a continuum between mild, moderate, severe and profound/multiple. The term 'learning difficulties' has in educational terms replaced 'educationally subnormal', and is increasingly used in favour of the label 'mental handicap'.

Students with special educational needs: Students who require additional support to facilitate learning.

GUIDE TO ABBREVIATIONS

ABE: Adult Basic Education
DES: Department of Education and Science
ERA: Education Reform Act
FEU: Further Education Unit
HMI: Her Majesty's Inspectorate
LEA: Local Education Authority
NBSD: National Bureau for Students with Disabilities (now known as Skill)
NIACE: National Institute of Adult Continuing Education

USEFUL ADDRESSES

Adult Literacy and Basic Skills Unit
Kingsbourne House
229—231 High Holborn
LONDON WC1V 7DU
Tel: 071 405 4017
Newsletter and publications on adult basic education.

Arts Council
105 Piccadilly
LONDON W1V 0AU
Tel: 071 629 9495
Publishes a directory of arts projects and organisations
working with people who have disabilities.

Barnardo's
Tanners Lane
Barkingside
ILFORD
Essex IG6 1QG
Tel: 081 550 8822
Information and advice; regional projects for adults
with learning difficulties offer some training
opportunities.

British Epilepsy Association
40 Hanover Square
LEEDS LS3 1BE
Tel: 0345 089 599
Practical help, counselling, public education, action
groups.

British Institute of Mental Handicap
Wolverhampton Road
KIDDERMINSTER
Worcestershire DY10 3PP
Tel: 0562 850251
Journal *Mental Handicap* (quarterly), *Mental Handicap
Research* (biannual), *Current Awareness Service*
(monthly bibliography), information on courses,
regional groups.

Castle Priory College
Thames Street
WALLINGFORD
Oxfordshire OX10 0HE
Tel: 0491 37551
Short courses with a national catchment.

Community Care
Carew House
WALLINGTON
Surrey SM6 0DX
Tel: 081 661 4861/4699
Social work magazine.

Community Living
Hexagon House
Surbiton Hill Road
SURBITON
Surrey KT6 4TZ
Tel: 081 390 9393
Magazine on the theme of developing high-quality
services for people with learning difficulties.

CMHERA
c/o Paul Williams
69 Wallingford Road
GORING
Oxfordshire RG8 0HL
Tel: 0491 873522
PASS/PASSING workshops and evaluations.

Disability Alliance
25 Denmark Street
LONDON WC2H 8NJ
Tel: 071 240 0806
Publishes the *Disability Rights Handbook*; provides
advice/information/campaigns on social security
benefits for people with disabilities.

Disabled Living Foundation
380—384 Harrow Road
LONDON W9 2HV
Tel: 071 289 6111
Advice and information on equipment and aids for
daily living. By appointment, people can look at and
try some of the 2000 pieces of equipment available.

Down's Syndrome Association
153—155 Mitcham Road
Tooting, LONDON SW17 9PG
Tel: 081 682 4001 (24-hour)
Offers information, advice, support and counselling for
people with Down's Syndrome, their carers, interested
professionals and others.

Further Education Unit
Grove House
2 Orange Street
LONDON WC2H 7WE
Tel: 071 321 0433
Publications and information relating to the
development of further education.

King's Fund Centre
126 Albert Street
LONDON NW1 7NF
Tel: 071 267 611
Publications based on health service developments for
people with learning difficulties.

MENCAP National Centre
123 Golden Lane
LONDON EC1Y 0RT
Tel: 071 454 0454
Support and help for parents; residential services;
training and employment services, leisure facilities;
courses for staff; legal and information services;
conferences and campaigns. Publishes *Mencap News*
(monthly) and a book catalogue *Mencap Books.*

National Association of Teachers in Further Higher
Education (NATFHE)
15—27 Britannia Street
LONDON WC1X 9JP
Tel: 071 837 3636
Trade union and professional association.
*NATFHE Journal, Journal of Further and Higher
Education.* Specialist subject sections include special
educational needs and adult basic education.

National Autistic Society
276 Willesden Lane
LONDON NW2 5RB
Tel: 081 451 1114
Advice and guidance to professionals and families;
journal *Communication*; training courses and seminars.

National Citizen Advocacy
2 St Paul's Road
LONDON N1 2QR
Tel: 071 359 8289
Advice, information and publications.

National Council for Educational Technology
Sir William Lyons Road
Science Park
University of Warwick
COVENTRY CV4 7EZ
Information on micro-electronics.

National Council for Special Education
1 Wood Street
STRATFORD UPON AVON
Warwickshire CV37 6JE
Tel: 0789 205332
Education charity promoting education for children
and young adults with special educational needs.
Publishes the *British Journal of Special Education*
(quarterly).

National Institute of Adult Continuing Education
19B De Montfort Street
LEICESTER LE1 7GE
Tel: 0533 551451
Advice and information on adult education, journal
Adults Learning (monthly), publications list on request.

NIACE REPLAN
Central Unit
NIACE
19B De Montfort Street
LEICESTER LE1 7GE
Tel: 0533 551451
Regional field officers promote the development of
educational opportunities for unemployed adults.

NIACE Rowntree Project
Charles Street Adult Education Centre
Charles Street
LUTON LU2 0EB
Tel: 0582 22566
From 1990—1992 a programme of conferences will
disseminate the findings of the NIACE Rowntree
Project 'Continuing Education for Adults with
Learning Difficulties', of which this handbook is a
result.

The Open University
Walton Hall
MILTON KEYNES
MK7 6AA
Tel: 0908 274066
The Department of Health and Social Welfare offers a number of courses related to people with learning difficulties.

People First
National Office
Oxford House
Derbyshire Street
LONDON E2 6HG
Tel: 071 739 3890
Self advocacy network; *Newsletter.*

RADAR
25 Mortimer Street
LONDON W1N 8AB
Tel: 071 637 5400
Information and advice for people with physical disabilities. Publications, fact sheets, campaigns.

The Rathbone Society
1st Floor
Princess House
105—107 Princess Street
MANCHESTER M1 6DD
Tel: 061 236 5358
Voluntary organisation offering information, advice and provision for people with moderate learning difficulties.

Shape
1 Thorpe Close
LONDON W10 5XL
Tel: 081 960 9245
Network creating arts opportunities for adults with disabilities.

Skill: National Bureau for Students with Disabilities
(Formerly National Bureau for Handicapped Students)
336 Brixton Road
LONDON SW9 7AA
Tel: 071 274 0565

Voluntary organisation developing opportunities for students with special educational needs in continuing education. Journal *Educare*, publications, advice, regional groups.

Spastics Society
12 Park Crescent
LONDON W1
Tel: 071 387 9571
Publishes *Disability Now* newspaper. Central information unit.

Special Needs Research Unit
Newcastle upon Tyne Polytechnic
Coach Lane Campus
1 Coach Lane
NEWCASTLE UPON TYNE
NE7 7TW
Tel: 091 235 8211
Research, design and consultancy unit on information technology and special educational needs. Databases and publications.

Unit for the Development of Adult Continuing Education (UDACE)
Christopher House
94B London Road
LEICESTER LE2 0QS
Tel: 0533 667252
UDACE examines areas of possible development in the education of adults and recommends strategies for development. A publications list is available.

Values Into Action (VIA)
(formerly Campaign for People with Mental Handicaps, CMH)
Oxford House
Derbyshire Street
LONDON E2 6HG
Tel: 071 729 5436
Newsletter, annual conference, normalisation workshops, publications.

Values Into Action Publications
5 Kentings
Comberton
Cambs CB3 7DT

Index